TAKE ME HOME

BINDARRA CREEK A TOWN REBORN

SUZANNE GILCHRIST

MALLEE STAR ENTERPRISES

S. E. Gilchrist can't remember a time when she didn't have a book in her hand. Now she dreams up stories where her favourite words are ... 'what if' and 'where'? Writing as both S. E. Gilchrist and Suzanne Gilchrist, she loves combining romance with adventure and suspense across many different genres including science fiction/space opera, apocalyptic, and contemporary small towns.

For more information, visit her website:
www.segilchrist.com

ALSO BY THE AUTHOR

Writing as: SUZANNE GILCHRIST

Cowboy under the Mistletoe (Edge of the Outback Romance)
Dance in the Outback (Edge of the Outback Romance)
The Cowboy's Gift (Edge of the Outback Romance)
Under an Outback Sky (Edge of the Outback Romance)
Love's Sweet Challenge (Bindarra Creek Short & Sweet)
Take Me Home (Bindarra Creek A Town Reborn)
A Dangerous Secret (Bindarra Creek Mystery Romance)
The Mistletoe wish (Bindarra Creek Christmas Romance)
The Glitter or The Gold (Bindarra Creek Small Town Christmas)

Writing as: S. E. GILCHRIST

SCIENCE FICTION / SPACE OPERA ROMANCE
Darkon Warriors series:
Legend Beyond the Stars
The Portal
Awakening the Warriors
Star Pirate's Justice
When Stars Collide
Bargain with the Enemy
Touring the Stars

The Slave Trap

Mars Academy Series:

Stranded

Cosmic Fire

APOCALYPTIC ROMANCE

Paying the Forfeit (Search for Home)

Storm of Fire (Search for Home)

Quest for Earth (Search for Home)

Don't Look Back (Warders of Earth)

CONTEMPORARY / SMALL TOWN ROMANCE

Bindarra Creek Makeover (A Bindarra Creek Romance)

Cotton Field Dreams (A Mindalby Outback Romance)

CONTEMPORARY ROMANTIC SUSPENSE

Scent of the Jaguar (A Deadly Forces Romance)

Endangered Heart

FANTASY/ANCIENT WORLDS EROTIC ROMANCE

Bound by Love

Bound by Lies

Take Me Home
Copyright © 2019 Suzanne Gilchrist
ISBN: 978-0-6484510-8-2

All Rights Reserved
Suzanne Hamilton

The right of Suzanne Hamilton writing as S. E. Gilchrist/Suzanne Gilchrist to be identified as the author has been asserted under the *Copyright Amendment (Moral Rights) Act 2000.*

Cover Design by: Patti Roberts of Paradox Book Design
Editor: Lauren of Creating Ink

Without limiting the rights under copyright above no part of this book may be reproduced or transmitted in any form or by any means, electronic or mechanical, including photocopying, recording, or by any information storage and retrieval system, without permission in writing from the author. Thank you for respecting the hard work of this author.

This is a work of fiction. Names, characters and incidents depicted in this book are the products of the author's imagination or are used fictitiously. Any resemblance to actual events, locales, organisations, or persons, living or dead, is entirely coincidental and beyond the intent of the author.

The author acknowledges the copyrighted or trademarked status and trademark owners mentioned in this work of fiction.

Mallee Star Enterprises, Queensland Australia

Written in Australian English

Author website: www.segilchrist.com

For my wonderful children, Kerstie, Kyle and Blake – follow your dreams and live each moment.

For my mother for her courage and strength.

CONTENTS

Chapter 1	1
Chapter 2	11
Chapter 3	16
Chapter 4	25
Chapter 5	32
Chapter 6	45
Chapter 7	50
Chapter 8	54
Chapter 9	59
Chapter 10	68
Chapter 11	74
Chapter 12	87
Chapter 13	93
Chapter 14	100
Chapter 15	105
Chapter 16	115
Chapter 17	120
Chapter 18	129
Chapter 19	140
Chapter 20	151
Chapter 21	159
Chapter 22	168
Chapter 23	176
Chapter 24	182
Chapter 25	192
Chapter 26	199
Chapter 27	205
Chapter 28	214
Chapter 29	223
Chapter 30	232
Epilogue	240

Bindarra Creek Romance series   245
Acknowledgments   248

CHAPTER 1

The icy winter night closed in around the paddy wagon, the instant Senior Constable Abigail Taylor killed the engine. Shivering as the heater died and the gusty wind rocked the car on its axles, she pulled her navy-blue beanie over her blonde hair then glanced across at Senior Sergeant Riley Morgan.

"Looks like we have company." Abby nodded to where three figures could be seen, shoulders hunched in their winter coats, hands deep in their pockets, as they stamped their feet on the front porch of Bindarra Creek Police Station.

The security lighting did little to discern their features, hidden beneath hoods pulled low over their faces. An adult and a couple of kids, thought Abby, as she took a sharp visual inventory. The kids kept their backs to the adult, standing a good three metres away as if to emphasise they didn't belong as a unit. Possibly an irate homeowner who had caught the kids in the act of desecrating his fence with graffiti - all in the name of art - or boredom.

More paperwork. More soothing of ruffled feathers. More kids to place on 'clean-up' duty. She bit back her sigh, her hopes of catching the bistro at the Riverside Pub before it closed, disappearing like Halley's Comet over the horizon.

Riley rubbed a hand over his stubbly jaw and mumbled past a wide yawn, "I'll see to it."

Smiling, Abby released her seat belt and slipped the keys from the ignition. "Nope. Leave it to me, boss. You've got a full night ahead of you with that baby of yours."

"Teething!" He groaned. "Never thought baby teeth could cause so much pain."

Ignoring the savage momentary twist of jealousy that gripped her, Abby managed a grin. "For you or the kid?"

"All of us." Meeting her gaze, Riley grimaced. "I'm on night duty tonight while Sam gets some sleep."

"All the more reason for me to deal with whoever is on our front doorstep."

"Thanks. I'll give you a hand, writing up tonight's incident in the morning."

"Sounds like a plan." Eager to avoid any more talk about children, Abby grabbed her thick police-issue jacket from the back of the seat while Riley climbed out the other side of the wagon.

With a brief wave, she pushed open the car door then leaned heavily against it as the wind slammed it back toward her body. "Ouch. I'll be so glad to get out of this weather."

"You okay?" Riley placed his hand on the bonnet.

"Yeah, all good. Thanks. See you bright and early." She

pushed her arms into the sleeves of her jacket while Riley sprinted towards the highway patrol car and climbed inside.

A few moments later, his car's taillights disappeared down the road – heading for home. Heading for a hot dinner that was no doubt waiting for him. But definitely heading home to his family.

Family. Something Abby no longer had in her life.

Burying her brief flash of sadness, she turned to the small group waiting for her. With her hands resting lightly on her gel duty belt, she strode the short distance through a buffeting wind so cold it made her eyes water and her nose numb. She lifted her gaze briefly to the dark sky where clouds scudded across the scattering of stars. Too high to portend any rain, unfortunately. The region could do with a good downfall. But an early morning frost could well be on the cards. In other words, a very chilly night.

Flexing her stiff fingers, she stopped on the top step, her heart doing a crazy skip as she recognised the adult. "Elizabeth! What are you doing here?"

"At the moment, trying to keep warm." Elizabeth shuddered. "That wind is so cold."

"Tell me about it. I've just spent the past hour walking around the cemetery searching for non-existent burglars." Abby switched her stare to the two kids, both boys. The taller, was about thirteen or fourteen with a surly, belligerent twist to his mouth, and the other judging by his similar features, was his younger brother. Dark red hair that needed cutting, straggled about their pale, lightly freckled faces. "Who's this?"

"Kids who need your help. I've never forgotten your adoption application, Abby."

"Shame it was never approved." Attempting to act unconcerned, she took another inventory over the scene. Her hands clenched, bitter disappointment scorching her throat and she had to swallow hard over the sudden constriction. She'd thought she'd dealt with it – moved on. Apparently, the past still had the power to cut her to the bone.

"What can I do for you?" She straightened her shoulders as she brushed past the other woman, intending to unlock the door.

"Oh, we're not here on police business." Elizabeth gave a little laugh. It sounded forced.

Eyes narrowed, Abby swung around to face her. "Then why? I haven't heard from you in over four years."

The older woman shuffled her feet. "Can't we go somewhere warmer to talk? Where do you live?"

Abby's stomach grumbled, and she admitted, "I could do with some food. Have you eaten?"

"Yes. We stopped for dinner in Tamworth so we're fine. I'm parked across the road. How about I drive you home? I'd prefer if we were somewhere private and not inside a police station."

Abby recalled her nearly bare pantry and bit back a sigh. She'd have to make do with whatever was left in the cupboard – which was probably very little. For Elizabeth to appear out of the blue, whatever had happened had to be serious. Despite herself, Abby's pulse picked up and tension cramped her belly. "Thanks, but I'm on call and need to take the paddy wagon."

"Then we'll follow you." Elizabeth smiled.

Abby knew that serene look. It masked an iron will. Elizabeth wouldn't explain until she was good and ready. Bowing to the inevitable, she muttered, "Let's go then." She waited while Elizabeth shepherded the two boys across the road and into a white Holden sedan, not moving towards her own vehicle until she heard the other car's engine start.

A few minutes later, Abby drove along Mount Ingalls Road heading to the western section of town. She crossed over Gillies Bridge, and checked the rear vision mirror, noting the following headlights. Her mind teemed with questions while she battled not to acknowledge that stupid and forlorn hope that had refused to die.

Why was Elizabeth here? Was there a chance her adoption application's rejection had been overturned? But if so, why now? After all these years?

And what did those boys have to do with anything?

There were no street lights out here. The road was tarred, single lane and wide with the houses on both sides sitting on either one or several acres of land. Many had large sheds and out-buildings, but few lights shone between curtains drawn tight to shut out the wintry night.

She slowed as she neared the bend, flicked her indicator on to the left then turned off onto a narrow dirt road that led over a cattle grid.

A single light glowed on her verandah and pooled over the front of the house, proving the timer she'd had installed recently had been a good investment. Her car bumped down the driveway, before she pulled up near the steps. After turning off the engine, she exited, smiling as she caught the excited yaps of her tiny dog, Pinky, coming from inside.

Home.

No one rushed to greet her. No lights flicked on to welcome her. Only her dog waited.

Without looking at the small group piling from the other car, Abby unlocked the front door and took time to scoop Pinky into her arms and give her some attention. She then placed her gently onto the ground, and the little dog dashed onto the patchy, dry grass to relieve herself.

"Well, this looks nice." Elizabeth approached, beaming. She stooped to stroke the dog's head. "Good boy."

"She's a girl." Abby pushed the door wider, and whistled.

Pinky trotted up the steps.

Yawning, the two boys trooped through the door, banging it against the wall.

Both boys carried bulging backpacks and holdalls, and she frowned. Just what was Elizabeth up to?

"Is that a rat?" asked the eldest, pointing to Abby's small dog. A sneer curled his mouth.

"No, she's a Chihuahua and her name's Pinky. You have to be very gentle with her as she is so small, and her bones are quite delicate."

He jerked his gaze away and stared at the wall.

"I like dogs." The youngest boy sank to his heels and reached out a tentative hand to pat Pinky on the head. "We were never allowed to have a pet – 'cause of where we lived."

"That's a shame." She hesitated then added, "I've also got a horse called Geronimo and lots of ducks live down near the dam."

"Cool." He grinned.

But his smile faded when his older brother poked him in the back. "Come on, Eddie. Move."

Abby clicked her fingers and Pinky raced ahead into the kitchen. She indicated the room to the right and entered the lounge room on the heels of the two kids.

"Have you been here long?" Elizabeth asked as she followed Abby.

"Since I moved to Bindarra Creek almost three years ago. It's a rental," she added as the other woman took in the startling wall-paper of multi-coloured hibiscuses peeping amid lime-green palm fronds. "I like it because I've got a barn for Geronimo. He's getting on now and really feels the winters in his joints."

"I remember you talking about your horse."

Abby nodded. "Cuppa? What about you boys? Would you like a hot chocolate?"

With luck, there's sufficient milk to make one!

The younger one gave his brother a quick look before flinging himself onto the chaise.

"Yeah," said the older boy, obviously the spokesperson for the two, his voice grudging.

Wonderful. Just what I need after a long day chasing my tail. A kid with attitude. Abby shrugged out of her police jacket, hung it on a peg on the wall before crossing the room to turn on the gas heater. "The telly's remote is on the coffee table."

She walked into the kitchen, listening as Elizabeth admonished the boys to behave. Any further conversation was drowned out by the sudden blare of the TV.

Abby flicked on the electric kettle and set about making hot drinks. A quick glance inside the refrigerator revealed a quarter of a loaf of wholemeal bread, a few slices of cheese and one withered tomato. And little else, apart from half a litre of milk. A toasted cheese and tomato sandwich would have to do for her dinner, but at least she could give the kids a hot drink. Hating shopping, she always left it to the last minute before replenishing her shelves. However, she always ensured she had plenty of dog food.

She filled Pinky's bowls, one with dry biscuits and the other with a tin of premium tuna and rice, one of Pinky's favourites. Smiling, Abby watched as her dog tucked in, tail wagging furiously.

Elizabeth entered the room and dragged out a chair to sit at the small dining table. Placing her handbag neatly beside her feet, she drew a deep breath. "I know you have questions."

"Like about twenty," Abby muttered as she filled the waiting mugs with hot water. "Let's start with the most important one. Why are you here?"

"Them." Elizabeth shot a quick glance towards the living room then fixed her pale eyes on Abby's face, as if gauging her reaction. "I need you to look after them."

"What? Like fostering?" Abby frowned. "You know my situation. Roman and I are no longer together. And besides, teenagers or even younger kids were never what we wanted, which is why we didn't apply to be foster carers."

"I know." Elizabeth's voice dropped, became warm and emphatic. "You wanted a baby."

Despite her best efforts to remain unmoved by that precious word, tears filled Abby's eyes. She yanked open the cupboard to find the chocolate powder.

"I'm so sorry your application never eventuated."

Blinking hard, Abby spoke through her clenched teeth. "Yeah, well, you know why we were refused. Roman left me."

Elizabeth shook her head. "That wasn't the only reason. Many single parents are accepted these days. Did you end up re-applying? I've known several applicants who kept applying over many years before they were eventually approved."

"No. I wanted it all, a husband, a baby. After years of failing to conceive, and then having our application refused, I was a bit of an emotional wreck especially after I discovered one of the checks into our background failed."

Elizabeth sighed. "Don't forget that hit him hard too, Abby. It was a difficult time for him."

"I got that, but it wasn't the issue. His job sent him to that earthquake disaster in Nepal, but he never came back to me. How can I forgive that?" She bit down savagely on her lower lip as the memories flooded back.

The devasting results of lengthy tests after fruitless years of trying for a baby. What were the odds they were both infertile? Not even IVF was an option. Then their adoption application was rejected and Roman said he'd had enough, couldn't deal with another ride on the emotional roller coaster their lives had turned into.

Hands shaking, she dipped her spoon into the container. Chocolate powder spilled over the counter. She placed her hands palm down, and leaned into the cupboard. *Get a grip, Abby.* All this had happened years ago. It was time she pulled herself together. Breathing hard, she poured the hot water into mugs.

"I didn't say that you should forgive him, sweetie." Elizabeth paused before asking, "Is there someone new in your life?"

"No." Picking up the spoon, she stirred the hot drink savagely. At first, she'd been too busy so she couldn't think, wouldn't remember, concentrating on making a new future for herself – a life far, far different from what she'd dreamed it would be. A life alone. And now? Well now she was too busy living that life. A point she made a habit of reminding herself the second she woke every morning.

"You're almost forty."

"Nice of you to remind me." Abby swallowed, feeling the muscles along the line of her shoulders tighten like ropes. "No hope for me to ever hold my baby in my arms."

"But you can still have a child."

Abby turned around and leaned against the cupboards, saying harshly, "If you're thinking of those two delinquents in the lounge room, think again."

But Elizabeth slapped the table with her hand. "I *am* thinking of them. I need more than someone to be their mother – I need a cop I can trust. A cop who'll protect them – no matter what."

Abby froze. "Elizabeth, exactly what kind of trouble have you brought to my door?"

CHAPTER 2

The wind wailed against the windows, the glass rattling, the drawn curtains moving slightly with each blast. In her snug basket not far from Abby's feet, Pinky, clad in a sunshine-yellow, woolly dog jumper, shivered and curled herself tighter. From the living room, came the sounds of some action movie. Abby frowned, shooting a glance towards the doorway. Should she check what the boys were watching? Or leave it up to Elizabeth?

At the moment her former friend appeared more interested in sipping her hot tea than offering any explanation.

But that was Elizabeth. She liked to take her time to get to the point – a habit Abby had found frustrating at first until she'd realised Elizabeth used the tactic to gather more information before she finally came around to whatever she wanted to discuss.

Taking a seat opposite, Abby took a bite from her sandwich, no longer feeling hungry but knowing she needed the fuel. She'd use Elizabeth's approach and see what she could discover. "Are you still working in the child services field?"

"Not quite. I'm working with a facility that provides a refuge for victims of domestic violence. I love it. It's full on but I really feel like I'm making a difference," the older woman said.

She'd aged in the years since their last meeting – a meeting that had shattered all Abby's dreams of a family.

Abby did some mental maths. Elizabeth had to be in her mid-fifties now. Her cheeks had sagged, her faced was lined, and her bobbed hair almost completely grey. But determination still blazed from her eyes with the same zeal Abby remembered. After that gut-wrenching meeting, they'd spoken once or twice over the phone during the course of a few months, and then nothing for several years.

"How did you find me?" Abby poured the last of the milk, a few drops, into her mug.

"I've still got your parents' address. It did take some persuasion for them to tell me what I needed to know. Do they still run the farm?"

"Yeah, although Dad now employs a jackaroo to help him with the sheep. His arthritis is getting worse."

"Poor man, but he sounds like he's not ready to retire."

"I doubt he ever will. He loves everything to do with being a grazier. I can't see him leaving Dubbo anytime soon."

"And your mother?"

"She's just as keen as Dad to stay."

"That's good. Although I can only imagine how hard life is with this drought."

Abby grinned. "You're still good at dodging answers you don't want to give until you're ready."

"It's a difficult subject. Unfortunately, I can't tell you a great deal." Averting her gaze, Elizabeth sighed as she set her mug onto the table.

Abby lifted an eyebrow. "Can't or won't?"

"Both," the other woman said bluntly. She lowered her voice. "The boys' parents are dead. Their father died some years past and their mother passed away thirteen months ago. They were placed into care, but no foster home was able to handle them."

"Wonderful. So you thought of me."

"Not then. It wasn't until I received a letter from their mother four months ago - via a public executor actually that I found out they existed." Elizabeth stared off into the middle distance. Her mouth trembled then firmed. "I knew her. She was Brian's youngest cousin. But I never knew she was suffering from terminal cancer. I wasn't even informed when she died."

Brian. Elizabeth's deceased husband. Abby had never met him and although Elizabeth had rarely mentioned him, she'd gained the impression the marriage had been one of those rare instances of two soul mates finding each other.

Like me and Roman.

Abby quickly buried the thought and stared hard at the older woman. "Did you know she had children?"

"No. We weren't invited to the wedding. No one in Brian's family was and when I asked around, no one had heard from her since she left home when she was eighteen."

Abby frowned. "Sounds like you weren't close."

"After Brian died my social work became everything

to me." Elizabeth shrugged. "I guess I allowed my former friends and family to drift away. Cathy had disappeared from our lives years before and I'd only met her a couple of times. I remember her as a sixteen-year old with this lovely red hair. That's how long it's been."

Elizabeth met Abby's sharp gaze. "In her letter, Cathy begged me to find a loving, protective home for her boys if she should die while they were still young. She stressed the word 'protective' by writing it in capital letters."

Abby stirred her tea while eyeing her companion carefully. It wasn't like Elizabeth to over-dramatise a situation, in fact the woman often struck Abby as someone with little imagination. Hinting at some kind of a conspiracy was totally out of character.

Of course, she was getting on.

Like someone else she knew.

Abby's thoughts winged back to the events of that evening when Reverend Miller had phoned the police station insisting a criminal was attempting to enter the locked church. The second such call this week, and the second time she and Riley had patrolled the church and cemetery for well over an hour. The second time, they'd found no evidence of a break-in, no evidence of anyone lurking in the bushes - nothing period. "How old are they?"

"Drew is fourteen while Eddie is almost eleven and a half."

Abby shot a glance towards the lounge room. The television had fallen silent. Were the boys listening or had they fallen asleep? She pushed to her feet, bidding Pinky to stay when the little dog lifted her head, then moved to the doorway. The boys were lying on her newly purchased stone-coloured six-seater corner chaise she had yet to find time to enjoy.

Abby walked over. Sound asleep, the younger boy didn't move as she pulled off his shoes before covering him with a blanket she took from the arm of the chaise. She looked up to find the older one, Drew, watching her. He appeared tense as if about to spring or push her away.

"Shoes please," she said firmly.

The kid nodded, kicked off his shoes then squeezed his eyes shut.

Abby took another blanket from the linen closet in the hall before coming back and placing it over his stiff body. He didn't relax or utter a word.

She switched the heater up a notch then turned to find Elizabeth standing in the doorway watching.

"See? You'll make a great mother." Elizabeth nodded.

"Don't get your hopes up." Abby walked into the kitchen and dropped into her chair. Picking up her mug, she swallowed the last of her now cold tea. "What do you want from me?"

"I need you to look after them. Keep them safe." Elizabeth's voice was fierce. "I need you to discover if they really are in danger. Then I need you to make it go away."

CHAPTER 3

The early morning sun cracked over the horizon spreading beams of amber across the landscape, when Roman Taylor pulled up outside his estranged wife's house.

He took his time, getting a good look at where she'd run to, absorbing the faded paint job on the old weatherboard house, the sagging wire fences, the straggling brittle weeds that passed for grass, the cracked, water-starved earth. But he could see the beauty in the place, too.

The tree-filled rolling hills to the east and north, and the undulating pastures dotted with tall eucalypts and grazing cattle, a couple of horses and a mob of kangaroos. The air filling his lungs, was crisp and clear. The sound of bird song and the flurry of wings as a flock of white cockatoos sailed over his head flying towards the glint of water that signalled a dam close by, were a balm to his strung-out nerves. In the distance, the windmill on its banks was a blur of motion as the icy wind cut across the land and stung his face.

Damn, it was cold.

Flexing his shoulders, he pulled off his woollen gloves then rubbed the back of his taut neck. It had been as stiff as concrete ever since he'd received that strange phone call from Elizabeth Ryder. Something was up.

Or rather, something was off.

He mounted the steps of the verandah then paused, his hand hovering a few centimetres from the door.

What would Abby say when she saw him? It had been five years since he'd said goodbye. Five years since he'd turned his back on his family or rather, on Abby.

The dreams they'd shared.

The heartbreak.

He heard the sounds of someone moving around. The clink of crockery, the bubbling of a boiling kettle. Then the skittering of claws over timber floorboards before a dog began to bark.

Regardless of his misgivings about the logic of being here, he knocked.

"Sit Pinky."

He hissed in a breath. Abby's low, husky voice still retained the power to stir him. His gut clenched as she opened the door.

"Roman?"

He drank her in – curly blonde hair to her shoulders, clear skin and a pair of light green eyes that always made him think of crystals glinting under water. She was already dressed for work in her police uniform sans boots. A tiny white Chihuahua in a yellow dog jumper sat at her feet, tail wagging, pink tongue hanging out.

That was new.

"What are you…?" Abby's eyes narrowed. She glanced

back over her shoulder then stepped outside, closing the door behind her. The dog moved with her, looking up at both of them before scampering off onto the grass. "It was Elizabeth, wasn't it? She called you."

"How are you, Abby?"

She folded her arms, her lovely mouth a straight line.

"She said you needed me." There it was three simple words, and yet they'd had the power to blast a hole in the protective wall he'd built around himself and send him racing to find her. He hadn't even asked why or what was going on. Simply packed an overnight bag and headed to the airport.

Abby raised her chin. "You needn't have bothered. She was wrong. I can handle this."

Pounding footsteps and yelling sounded from inside the house.

"You idiot! Where's my iPod?" roared an adolescent male voice.

"Hah! Try and find it!" squealed another male voice.

More pounding footsteps.

A door slammed shut.

The house seemed to shudder on its foundations.

Something else that was new.

His chest squeezed tight.

Abby's little dog went into a volley of frenzied barking and scampered back up the steps.

"She isn't used to the company yet," Abby said as she brushed past to gather the squirming dog into her arms. "Easy, Pinky, that's a good girl."

The dog stopped barking and began to pant. Abby planted a kiss on the Chihuahua's head before placing her onto the ground.

The dog pranced around Roman's feet, sniffing his hiking boots.

"What's her name again?" Roman smiled, his mind working overtime. Who else was inside the house, apart from kids? Was there another man in Abby's life?

"Pinky. You have a problem with that?" Her voice held more than a hint of challenge.

"It sounds like a great name." He spread out his hands, instantly dropping his gloves onto the ground.

Pinky pounced on them then dragged one off in her mouth. She raced along the verandah.

"Hey! Come back here."

"Too late. It's hers now." Abby smiled.

Finally. A tiny fissure in her cool composure.

Roman's shoulders sagged. "I could do with some breakfast."

Abby rolled her eyes. "You're always hungry. You'll be in good company. Those two inside have bottomless pits for stomachs. I've already been down to the twenty-four-seven servo in Corella to get more food."

"Still hate shopping?" He grinned then wished he'd bitten out his tongue as her smile died and her mouth tightened. Obviously, any references to their past shared life was taboo. That suited him fine. As soon as he was assured she was in no danger, then he would be out of there.

An awkward silence fell as she looked away. "I'll do a proper shop later." She flicked him a quick glance then nodded. "You'd better come in."

She called her dog.

Roman noted, with dismay, the animal returned minus his glove.

"Don't worry. I'll find it after breakfast." She led the way into the lounge room, her dog on her heels. "Drew! Eddie! There's someone I want you to meet."

Silence met her call.

Shrugging she walked into the kitchen and over to the stove. Seconds later, the delicious scent of sausages and onions filled the air.

Roman pulled gently at the dog's ears then went over to lean against the fridge. "Need a hand?"

"You can make toast. Try the fridge for the bread and butter."

"I'm all over it."

Abby cracked eggs into another pan while he attended to his task. They soon had several plates loaded with fried eggs, breakfast sausages and onions and a mound of buttered toast. But then, they'd always worked well as a team.

He looked up as footsteps hurried down the hall, probably drawn by the smell of food. Two red-haired boys burst into the room. Tension bled away as Roman recognised no familiarity in their features. Whoever they were, he would bet his last dollar they were no relation to Abby.

The shorter boy went to rush towards the table but the taller and skinnier one reached out and yanked the other boy to a halt. Fairly vibrating with suspicion, the older one darted his gaze between the adults.

"Let go, Drew. I'm hungry," the younger kid said, trying to pull away.

Abby spoke calmly, "It's okay. Drew and Eddie, this is my… my husband. Roman Taylor."

Roman placed the plates of food onto the table then

took a chair, taking care it was the farthest from where the boys stood.

Drew released his brother who immediately rushed over and sat down. The older boy took the place next to him, his expression watchful.

Roman gave him a short smile then turned his attention to Abby who was brewing coffee. She soon brought over two steaming mugs to the table and, after handing him one, sat down with a sigh.

"Long night," she said, glancing to where the boys were beginning to eat then back to meet Roman's stare.

"Who are they?"

"Elizabeth turned up last night, around nine thirty, with them in her car. She'd driven non-stop from Sydney to find me." Abby forked up some eggs and ate before continuing. "She wants me to look after the boys for a couple of weeks."

Foster kids? "What was the rush?"

She shook her head sharply, then lightly cleared her throat. A warning for him not to ask too many personal questions in front of them.

"Is Elizabeth still here?"

"I don't have any spare beds. The kids slept on the chaise. They'd fallen asleep by the time Elizabeth left so they stayed here. We didn't want to disturb them. I rang a local B&B and got Elizabeth a room for the night. As soon as we've eaten, I'll call and arrange for us to meet at the Cyprus Café. I still have a lot of unanswered questions," she said grimly.

"Same." Roman took a mouthful of his black coffee, welcoming the bitter taste and the rush of caffeine surging through his system. He could do with a few hours' sleep himself but perhaps it would be better to wait until after he'd spoken with Elizabeth. "I left Manila yesterday morning on the first flight I could get."

"It's…it's kind of sweet that you rushed so fast to see me." She fiddled with her fork.

He lowered his voice. "A lack of love was never our problem, Abby."

Her eyes glistened wetly as she whispered, "I know."

His hand covered hers and she trembled beneath his touch. Emotions swelled his chest so tight he thought he might burst. Words tangled in his throat. What to say? How to explain? And did she even want to hear his excuses anymore? Or was it all too late?

"She won't be there," said Drew, in a hostile tone.

The moment passed.

Roman dragged his gaze from Abby's face and looked over to where the older kid stared back, expression blank, eyes carefully cool.

Eddie placed his knife and fork onto the table, hugged his waist and ducked his head, like a kid who'd seen far too many violent arguments and was waiting for the fist to fall.

Just who the hell were these kids and where had they come from?

And why had Elizabeth brought them to Abby?

Drew flung himself back into his chair, a snarl curling his lips. "She'll be gone. Just like everyone else."

Acting unconcerned, Abby fed her little dog a small piece of egg. "Do you think so? I guess it's possible, but I know Elizabeth would only have left if she had a good reason. Let's call and find out."

"Whatever. I don't care. We're not staying here, and you can't make us."

"Legally, I can." Abby looked up and smiled. "I've got temporary foster papers all signed sitting in my sent emails. I had a very busy night. Listen, I know this isn't what either of you want but why not give it a go for a few weeks? There's lots to do here. You'll have fun."

Startled, Roman examined Abby's face but failed to read what she was thinking from her carefully controlled expression. Elizabeth must have used a powerful incentive for Abby to change her mind about fostering, especially older kids. Now, if it had been a baby, he could have understood.

His gut clenched as if someone had sucker punched him, and he had to clamp his mouth shut to cover his gasp.

Baby, another taboo word.

For both of them.

"It's crap. We're miles from anywhere. And this place is a dump." Drew jabbed a thumb over his shoulder.

"You're right, it does need a bit of attention." Abby looked in a thoughtful manner at the faded green and orange kitchen cupboards.

Drew looked uncertain, as if an adult had never listened to his opinion before.

"Then there's school," Abby continued to speak.

Aghast expressions spread over the kids' faces and faint amusement lifted Roman's dark thoughts.

"Also, there's scouts, horse-riding, football, kayaking, hiking…I could go on." She sat back and traded stares with the older boy.

A wide-eyed Eddie tugged at his brother's arm. "Drew. Drew. Did you hear? It sounds fun."

Drew shrugged him off but some of his belligerence fell away. "I guess we may as well stay. Until you're sick of having us around and get rid of us."

Poor kids. Must be hard being shunted from one place to the other, never experiencing the love of a real home. Always knowing that in a few days, a month, they'd be moved onto some place different. Roman took a mouthful of cold coffee.

"Finish eating your breakfast and after, both of you can wash up while I make some calls." Abby rose, obviously deciding not to respond to Drew's baited statement.

After throwing Abby a suspicious glance, Drew tucked into his meal while his brother downed a glass of milk.

Feeling somewhat bemused and more than a little unsettled, Roman also finished his breakfast.

Abby's list of activities did sound fun, a bitter-sweet reminder of what their life could have been, should have been.

He scrubbed a hand over his taut forehead, pushing away those troubling thoughts. Nothing he'd heard so far explained why Elizabeth had been so adamant Abby's life was in danger. Had the social worker's call been a ruse to attempt a reconciliation between them? Or was there more going on she had yet to divulge? If so, then his innate instinct for trouble told him those two kids were involved up to their necks.

Roman swallowed the last of his coffee and placed his empty plate in the sink. After nodding to the two boys, he left the kitchen.

It was time to find out what was going on.

CHAPTER 4

Hands shaking, Abby dealt with the first item on her 'must do' list; see if she could get the boys into school to give them a sense of stability and routine. That would give her some hours to process all that had happened.

Not the least being her husband turning up on her doorstep.

Honestly! What had Elizabeth been thinking?

She didn't need him. She'd made a life that didn't include him.

So why does my heart still stutter at the thought of him? My body melt and tremble at the sight of him?

Like Roman said, love had never been their problem.

She sat on the edge of her bed and tried the school principal's number again and finally got through. After explaining that she had two unexpected boys in her charge for a few weeks and that she needed to establish a routine as soon as possible, she received the okay to bring them to the school that morning. It would take around an hour for the orientation and completion of paperwork then if everything was satisfactory, the boys could attend classes for the remainder of the day.

Doing her best to smother the memory of Drew's heart-wringing words, Abby flicked through the folder Elizabeth had left and read out the boys' dates of birth before ending the call.

When Roman rapped on her door, she paused, and took a steadying breath then said, "Come in."

Her gaze swept over his well-built figure, admiring the natural grace of his walk before she looked down.

Focus, girlfriend. That part of your life is over.

She tapped the folder with her finger. "This is the information Elizabeth left regarding the boys. It has their birth certificates and immunisation history but little else. Nothing about their school grades or where they lived. And no photos. Not even a photo of their parents."

"You sound like you've decided to take them on."

"Honestly, Elizabeth didn't give me much of a chance to say no," Abby said slowly. Her voice held a hint of surprise as if she, too, was uncertain of her reasons. "I guess I feel sorry for them. They don't seem to have anywhere else to go." She shrugged. "They seem … lost."

"Don't forget hostile. Drew definitely isn't keen on authority figures."

Abby smiled then frowned. Why the heck did she keep hearing Drew's voice? *'Until you're sick of having us around and get rid of us.'* That was no way for any kid to live.

She made an effort to concentrate on the task at hand and met Roman's questioning eyes. "True. But I did stress, this is only a temporary arrangement. A few weeks, one month at the most, which is when the foster contract ends."

He settled beside her and reached for the folder. "May I?"

"Sure."

"The lack of photos isn't that strange, surely? If they're orphans, maybe no one bothered to take any photos of the kids."

"They've only recently been placed in foster care, Roman. Before their mum died, they lived with her. And Elizabeth distinctly mentioned the father died only a few years ago. I would have thought there'd be photos, even copies of awards, school reports, some memories of their past."

"Perhaps the guy who died was their stepfather or simply her partner at the time. And their biological dad was never on the scene. Either way, if the relationship wasn't happy, there could have been too many other challenges for the mother to cope, which may be why she didn't capture these kids' lives." He opened the folder and began to read through the contents.

"I guess that's a possibility." Abby twisted her wedding ring round on her finger. Should she mention everything Elizabeth had told her? She scrolled through her memory then reassured there was nothing there that could be construed as breaking a confidence, she told him about the conversation held the previous night. After finishing, she scrutinised his face. "What exactly did Elizabeth tell you?"

"That you were in danger. She never mentioned any kids."

"And yet she told me it was the boys who are in

danger." Abby hesitated then added, "This is *not* about me, Roman. It's some mess concerning the boys. No need for you to stay longer. You can return to your life and that amazing career of yours, satisfied that all is okay in my world." She gave a tight smile.

"Still flogging that dead horse about my job, Abby?" A tiny pulse beat beside his temple as he met her gaze. He blew out a breath, flexing his shoulders as if to reduce sudden tension. "I want answers, Abby. And until then, I'm not going anywhere. Have you called her yet?"

"I tried once and only got her answering service. I'll try again." Abby listened as the mobile rang and rang on the other end until eventually, Elizabeth picked up.

"Hello?"

"Elizabeth, it's Abby. Abby and Roman."

"Oh."

In the background Abby heard the sound of the radio playing and what sounded like road noise. She frowned and put the phone on speaker. "I've popped you on speaker, Elizabeth. Where are you?"

"I'm on my way back to Sydney. I need to get back to my job. I'm sorry, Abby. I know you wanted to talk but there is little more I can tell you. I don't have the means to hire a private investigator, which is why I thought of you."

In disbelief, Abby shook her head. "I don't believe it. You can't just dump these boys and disappear. Not so soon."

"I have to. It's better this way. Besides I'm not one hundred percent certain I wasn't followed to Bindarra Creek. You'll need to be careful, Abby."

Roman leaned closer. "Bloody hell! Elizabeth what's going on?"

"I wish I knew."

"What makes you think you're being followed?" Abby interjected.

"There was a car this morning outside Fig Tree Lodge with Victorian number plates. I swear it wasn't there last night when I went to bed."

"That could be anyone. Someone from interstate visiting relatives."

"Check it out then, Abby. It was a dark blue Lexus convertible. Now tell me a car like that is what you see every day in a small country town."

Abby pinched the bridge of her nose and sighed. "Probably not. Number plates?"

"Sorry, too far for me to see without my glasses. By the time I got back to the window with them, the car was gone."

"I'll do a drive around the town before work this morning and see if I can find it and let you know. I take it no one is following you now." Her voice was wry.

"Of course not. Don't you think I would have said? If I discover anything further, I'll call straight away, Abby. Take care. Both of you." Elizabeth rung off.

They sat in silence looking at each other.

Roman pushed to his feet. "That settles it. I'm not going anywhere until this matter is sorted. Okay if I take a shower?"

"Sure. There's spare towels in the closet." Abby plucked at the doona. "About the sleeping arrangements ... you could stay at Fig Tree Lodge Bed and Breakfast."

He scowled. "I prefer to stay here."

She shook her head. "Let's not confuse the issue. Besides I only have two bedrooms. I'll need to find a couple of beds and mattresses for the boys as it is …" Memories of sharing a bed with Roman flooded her mind and teased her body to life. She pressed a trembling hand to her belly.

"I originally thought I'd only be here for a day or two. Now, I'm not so certain we'll discover the problem so quickly." Wicked amusement glinted in his silver eyes. "About those sleeping arrangements …"

Sternly ignoring the instant softening of her body at the thought of those 'sleeping arrangements, she muttered, "I'm not going to change my mind."

"We'll see. If you or those boys really are in danger, there is no way I'll leave you in this house unprotected." His voice rang out, grim and determined. The heat in his eyes cooling.

"You could always stand on guard out the front. I can just see you marching to and fro."

He eyed her for a second then they both laughed.

Abby checked the time on her mobile then stood. "I need to get to work. As soon as you've showered, you can follow me into town to Fig Tree Lodge."

"What about the boys?"

"They can come with. We've got an appointment at the school at eleven a.m. If all goes as planned, they'll remain in school for the rest of the day while I'm at work."

"After I've extended the rental period of the car I've hired, I'll look into extra beds and stuff for you."

Abby hesitated, not liking how here he was, barely two hours arrived, and already inching his way into her life. But she couldn't deny her job was busy enough without adding additional chores to the list. "I don't have a trailer."

He shrugged. "No sweat. I'll lease one from the garage."

"All right. If you could sort the beds, that will be a big help. Try the 'For Sale' section of the local paper first. It's called the *Bindarra Bugle*. Then there's Dodge Myers' antique shop. If it's open. I understood Dodge was out of town for a few days. He could know where we can get our hands on some second-hand beds." She frowned. "Maybe I'll have to order on-line and get what I need delivered from Tamworth. But that will take a few days."

"Hey." His hand closed around her upper arm.

When had he moved so near?

Her breathing stumbled as she focused on the sexy stubble lining his firm jaw. It was salt and pepper, matching his tousled, short hair and quite distinguished against his olive skin and striking silver-grey eyes.

"Let it go, Abby. I said I'll deal with it."

Unable to speak, she nodded as for one heart-stopping moment she wondered whether he'd lean closer.

Maybe press a kiss on her lips.

Maybe wrap his strong arms around her.

Maybe …

Releasing her arm, he left the bedroom.

She sagged onto the bed and covered her face with her hands. What was she doing? In the space of a few hours, she'd taken on responsibility for a couple of young, homeless boys. And she'd accepted her soon-to-be ex-husband's offer to help.

The well-ordered, busy life she'd worked hard to attain these past few years had dissipated like the last puff of smoke from a fireless dragon.

What *had* she done?

CHAPTER 5

*A*bby did her best to ignore Senior Sergeant Riley Morgan as he pushed his keyboard aside then began to riffle through the incident reports in his tray.

"Abby?"

He's going to ask me about the kids I brought to the station this morning. How to answer? She continued to tap at the keyboard, writing up her account of the night before, knowing he must be bubbling over with curiosity. "Yeah, Sarge?"

"Err … "

From the corner of her eye, she watched him scratch his chin.

He cleared his throat. "Think there's anything in the good reverend's insistence he's about to be robbed?"

"The church. Not himself."

"I got the impression he considered there was no distinction between the two." Riley pinned her in place with his gaze. "Well?"

She remained still. "We've completed thorough

searches, both times. It's possible the perpetrator had disappeared by the time we got to the church."

"But you don't think so." His comment was more statement than question. He was waiting to hear if her thoughts about Reverend Jonas Miller aligned with his. After three years of working together, they could read each other fairly well.

She hit the save key. "You don't either. I think we should pay an unofficial visit to his wife."

Seated at the reception counter, probationary Constable Agwe (better known as AJ) Donaldson, fresh out of the police academy and only son of the local mayor, called out, "Ugh. Florence Miller. Lovely lady, but you know who she's best friends with, don't you?"

"Yes, AJ, I do. Edwina Lette."

"Mrs Lette had Sarge here, bailed up outside the bank the other day for a good half hour. What was she saying, Sarge? Telling your kid's fortune?"

Abby swallowed her giggle at Riley's aggrieved expression.

"*And* ..." AJ dragged out the single word dramatically. "She's best buddies with old Pamela Brown. She took a broom to me when I was a teenager. I was only after a couple of oranges."

This time, Abby laughed.

AJ grinned and tapped the side of his nose. "Remember what I told you, Senior Constable. If Edwina starts peering into your palm, run." AJ gave a mock shudder then took a sip of his coffee, merriment glowing in his dark eyes.

A smile tugging his lips, Riley slapped the folder shut. "Moving on, you two." He shot Abby a furtive look.

She resigned herself and waited.

"Now about those boys I saw you with this morning, Abby."

"It's a personal matter, Sarge. I'm simply looking after them for a few weeks."

His eyebrows lifted. "I also heard a rumour in the café this morning that you were seen about town with a strange bloke in tow."

Her face burned. "My ex-husband. Well, to be exact we haven't signed the divorce papers yet."

"You are a woman of mystery, Senior Constable."

"I try to be," she quipped back.

"I'm not surprised she's got a bloke in tow. She's hot, Sarge." AJ toasted Abby with his mug, his deep chocolate eyes twinkling.

"Careful, Constable," warned Riley.

AJ's grin vanished. His dark skin turning ruddy over his cheek bones, he ducked his head and began scribbling away. "Yes, sir. Sorry, Senior Constable."

Abby placed her hand over her mouth to hide her amusement from AJ. Young and eager for life, nothing seemed to dim his enthusiasm for his job, or his cheekiness.

Shaking his head, Riley looked at Abby. "I bet you've got a few personal matters to organise today. Take some hours off to get sorted. AJ and I'll handle the station. And while you're at it, see if you can catch up with the reverend's missus. I'm keen to hear her take on this mysterious burglar."

"No worries, boss. And thanks." She gathered her bag and jacket, then paused. "Oh, by the way, Sarge? You've got baby spit on your shoulder."

Grinning, she left him scowling and rubbing at his jacket with a handful of tissues. She left the station and drove down Willow Drive heading for Fig Tree Lodge. After pulling up outside, she fished her mobile from her pocket and rang Roman.

"I've got a couple of hours free. Do you want to meet up?" she asked.

"Love to. Hang on."

She heard the muffled sound of voices then Roman came back on.

"We can lunch here. I've just organised it. Edwina says to come through the front door, go along the hall, and the dining room is second on your left."

"I'll be there in a couple of minutes." Smiling, she rung off, imagining AJ's face when she told him. Personally, she'd always found Edwina Lette to be nothing more than a friendly, if overly-inquisitive old lady. She'd heard the mutterings, of course, about the woman's second sight but such an 'ability' was a phenomenon that simply did not exist for Abby.

She set the car in motion again and drove through the open front gates of Fig Tree Lodge, admiring the lush gardens and the sprawling majesty of the ancient fig tree standing in pride of place on the lawn. The house appeared as old as the tree, and, recently renovated, it projected an aura of solid comfort as well as history.

After pulling up alongside the wide, shady verandah she locked the paddy wagon and mounted the steps.

Roman was waiting for her inside the front foyer. "Happy days. Looks like the gang's all here."

"What does that mean, exactly?"

"A quite interesting portion of the town's most influential citizens await you." He grinned and winked.

"Sounds like it's going to be a fascinating lunch." She chuckled. "Lead on."

Following on his heels, she found herself inside a large wood panelled room with an exquisite crystal chandelier hanging from an intricately carved plaster ceiling. A magnificent dining table that could seat twenty people sat in the centre of the room on a rich, brocade rug. A fire crackled in the marble fireplace, and curled up on a plush, emerald green rug in front of it, a grey-muzzled red kelpie snuffled softly in his sleep. The room was warm despite its size, a welcome respite from the blustery conditions outside.

Her gaze swept around the occupants. Edwina Lette sat at the head of the table, her eyes bird bright as she examined Abby. On her right, sat a young woman with long dark hair and deep brown eyes. Tessa Myers. Abby had seen her about town a few times and once with her husband, Dodge who Abby knew from the SES meetings. Tessa was cradling a baby a few months old in her arms and blowing raspberries much to the kid's gurgling delight.

Abby quickly looked away.

On Edwina's left sat her crony, Mrs Pamela Brown, with a wizened old bloke with wispy white hair seated beside her. Abby was pleased to see that the reverend's wife was present as well as a middle-aged Asian woman with short black hair, dressed in a tight crimson dress and with a huge jade pendant hanging from a too-slender neck.

"Sit down Senior Constable. I guess I have to call you

that, since you're in uniform. Lovely for you to join us." Edwina indicated a chair with a regal sweep of her be-ringed hand. Her many bracelets jangled.

"It's very kind of you to have me for lunch."

"Oh, it's no problem for me. Lou's the one cooking up a storm in the kitchen. Do you know everyone here?" Edwina pointed around the table. "Pam. Roy. Gloria. Florrie. Tessa. Little Tilly. And that's Rufus snoring by the fire. This delicious man candy I think belongs to you."

"Not quite. Good morning, everyone." Face hot, Abby smiled around the table then addressed the Asian lady. "I think you're Mayor Donaldson's wife and AJ's mother? I've seen you in the distance but don't believe we've ever met."

"Ahhhh right. No, I do not know you." Dark eyes gave Abby the once over, before she added with a smile that transformed her gaunt face, "Call me Gloria. How is my son doing?"

"Eager and keen to learn. He's fitted in well." Abby smiled.

"He is a good boy, Senior Constable."

"Since this is an unofficial visit, please call me Abby. And this is my ... husband, Roman Taylor," said Abby, as both she and Roman took chairs next to each other.

"Excuse me." Tessa rose so abruptly, the china on the table rattled. Clutching her child close to her chest, she hurried from the room.

"Damn," said Edwina, looking at the empty doorway. She raised her voice, "Don't forget to eat, Tessa!"

Edwina stared back at Abby for one long moment before switching her gaze to Roman. "It's your surname. Brings back bad memories for her."

She wasn't the only one.

Abby clenched her jaw and said nothing. She fiddled with her glass of water, refusing to satisfy the old lady's curiosity.

Roman shrugged but his voice was wary when he said, "It's not an unusual name."

"We had a spot of bother here a few years ago. Some maniac with a stalking fetish for very young girls. Any relation to Jason Taylor?"

Heat then cold swept over Abby. Her breathing seized. Her chest tightened. Blackness fogged her mind. What would Roman say? The truth? Or some banal comment and change the subject?

"Uncle by marriage. Born Kevin Robinson, he changed his name after he married my aunt. We've had little to do with him," Roman bit out.

Abby squeezed her eyes shut, remembering the suave property developer currently residing in a maximum-security prison. Roman's unworldly aunt had died of an overdose soon after their wedding leaving her considerable estate to her new husband. His family believed Kevin or Jason Taylor as he came to be known by, was responsible for her death. There was no way Lorraine would have become addicted otherwise. They'd suspected he'd dragged her into the murky underworld of crime and drugs, but nothing could be proven.

Although short-lived, the marriage had been long enough to taint all of Roman's family and drag them under the microscope of the press until another 'juicy' story broke the news. And long enough to put an end to Abby and Roman's hopes of adoption.

Regardless of their own unblemished past, the connection to a suspected drug smuggler was too risky to garner an approval. Especially when years later, he'd been convicted of stalking and attempted child kidnapping.

Tessa's eldest child - her daughter Kaylee.

That had been the last nail in the coffin where Abby and Roman's hopes for a family of their own were concerned.

Edwina smiled. "Glad we've got that out in the open. Always wanted to ask since the moment you arrived in town. Tessa won't judge his sins on you once I let her know. She's a fine girl."

Head held high, Pamela looked over at Abby and Roman. "Anyone with a grain of sense can see you two are nothing like that horrible man."

"Oh gosh no." Florrie Miller clasped her hands together. "You look like such a lovely couple."

"Don't start to pray, for pity's sake," grumbled Edwina. Frowning, she rubbed her chest.

The usually amiable Florence managed a stern expression. "We must say grace before a meal."

"What meal? I can't see any sign of food yet." Edwina yelled, "Hoi! Lou! Warren! Stop canoodling in my kitchen and get the dinner on the table."

Gloria and the old guy, Roy, laughed and even the thin-lipped Pamela allowed a stiff smile to stretch her lips.

Abby's tension dissipated. No one had turned accusing eyes towards them. No whispers behind hands. She should have brought the matter of her connection with a convicted criminal out in the open earlier when Riley had offered her the job. But she'd been afraid she'd be cold-shouldered in such a close-knit community. Afraid her plans for a new life, a fresh start, would be dashed. Now, it would only be a matter of hours and the news would be all over the town. Hopefully, the rest of Bindarra Creek's inhabitants would be just as broad-minded and accepting as her current companions.

Beside her, Roman let out a long, slow breath. His shoulder brushed against hers, the touch simple and comforting.

Ignoring them, Edwina began patting her pockets. "Where did I…"

"You mustn't smoke," snapped Pamela, making a suggestive eye roll towards Abby.

"Now, now, don't get miffed, Pam. There's nothing wrong with my eye-sight. I can see there's a cop in the room."

Smoke? Surely the old lady doesn't smoke weed?

Abby smiled then took a sip of water.

"Besides, that's not what I was looking for." With a glint of wicked mischief twinkling in her eyes, Edwina pulled out a bottle of tablets and placed them down with a thump.

"Honestly, Edwina." Pamela pursed her lips and shook her head.

Another gust of wind rattled the windowpane.

Gloria gave a dramatic shiver. "I hate winter. The long, dark days only good for lots of reading by the fire."

"It's been raining for three days up on the tablelands." The words came out of Pamela's mouth like bullets.

Roy patted her hand.

Mystified, Abby wondered what was behind that reassuring gesture.

"But not here. Don't fuss, Pam." Edwina sat back and folded her arms. A spasm seemed to cross her face.

Florrie heaved a heavy sigh. "It would be lovely to see some serious rain in Bindarra. Heaven knows we could do with a good soaking."

"A soaking yes, but we don't want a flood."

"Pwush, Pam. You're letting your imagination run away with you." Scowling, Edwina picked up her fork and rapped the table counter.

Pamela muttered, "But this wind …"

"Is only wind. No rain. No need to get those knickers of yours in a knot." Edwina thumped the table with each word she spoke.

Pamela glared back at her old friend. "Don't tell me. You've been talking to Matilda again."

Edwina slumped back against her chair and raised a thoughtful gaze to the ceiling. "No. She's been quiet lately. I don't understand."

"That happens when you've been dead for a century." Pamela smirked like she'd scored a hit.

Abby and Roman exchanged mystified looks.

A serious expression on his face, the old guy leaned forward and glanced at them. "Matilda is a ghost. She used to live in this very house before she died of the Spanish Flu back in 1919."

"What rubbish, Roy. No one comes back from the dead." But this time Pamela's voice was softer. Pamela and Roy smiled at each other.

A budding romance between two old people? How lovely.

Abby sniffed the air, and her tummy rumbled as she looked towards the doorway.

The rich, mouth-watering scent of pea and ham-hock soup wafted into the room as Lou Myers, entered, bearing a large soup tureen between her hands. "Grubs up."

Her husband and Edwina's ex-son-in-law, Warren Myers, tramped in close behind her, holding large baskets stuffed with hot garlic and herbed bread. They placed the food on the table before taking their own seats and introducing themselves to Roman.

Edwina waved a hand around the table, adding, "Lou used to be the senior sergeant in town before she gave birth to twin boys. But you probably know that already. Where *are* my grandsons, Lou?"

"In bed. Asleep."

Edwina snorted. "Not for long, I wager. Those pair have enough energy to power this town's entire electrical needs."

"I know." Lou grinned at her husband. "They get it from their dad."

Warren laughed and nudged her arm.

Florrie Miller bowed her head, and everyone fell silent while she muttered a quick prayer of thanks.

"This smells delicious." Gloria sniffed the air then reached for the soup tureen.

Edwina piled three slices of garlic bread onto her plate and began to eat.

"Isn't garlic bread too rich for you? All that butter." Pamela took the tureen from Gloria then ladled soup into her bowl before passing it onto Roy.

"You should watch your nagging, Pam. Puts men off." Edwina winked at Roy who blushed profusely.

Edwina promptly stuffed a huge piece of bread into her mouth.

Pamela looked like a cat about to spit and hiss.

"I intend to have soup and, afterwards, a big slice of black forest cake with my coffee," Edwina continued, barely pausing for breath. She wiped her mouth with a napkin then looked at Abby as she picked up her spoon. "Florrie said you were seen in town with a couple of boys. I didn't know you had children. Do they live with your man candy?"

Beside her, Roman pushed his bowl aside.

Children. Abby swallowed hard. "No. They're foster kids." She eventually forced out before asking, "Do any of your guests own a Lexus?"

"No idea. Tessa will know. Why not go up to her room and ask?"

"Thank you. I'll do that after lunch." *And hopefully she'll allow me time to explain. I should have done it before now.*

Edwina coughed, sucked in a noisy breath then coughed again.

"Crumb stuck in your throat, Mum?" Warren came quickly around the table and rubbed Edwina's back as she continued to cough.

Abby tensed.

The old lady's face turned purple.

"I think something's wrong." Abby surged to her feet.

"It's her heart!" Pamela cried out. "Breathe, Edwina!"

A horrified Florrie Miller placed her hands over her mouth and looked as if she was about to burst into tears.

Warren reached for the tablets and shook a pill into his palm. "Mum! Can you swallow this?"

But the old lady shook her head madly and turned aside, gasping and wheezing for breath, her fisted hands clutching at her chest.

"I'll call the doctor." Warren pulled out his mobile.

"There's no time. We need an ambulance," Abby said as Edwina, eyes rolling up into her head, crumpled sideways.

Warren dropped his phone to catch his mother-in-law. "It's okay, Mum. I've got you."

Florrie started to pray while Roy placed an arm around Pamela, who appeared frozen in her chair.

"I'll call for an ambulance." Abby clicked on her two-way radio which hung from her belt. "AJ, we have a situation. Ambulance required at Fig Tree Lodge. Suspected heart attack. And hurry."

CHAPTER 6

Abby paced to the front door of Fig Tree Lodge and stared at the empty drive before clicking on her two-way. "What's taking so long?"

"Ambo is tied up at a car crash out near Glenmeer," Riley responded. "AJ and I are on our way to the site now."

"Damn. That's twenty minutes away." Abby rubbed her forehead, spinning around when someone touched her shoulder.

Roman stood there, his face grave. "She's still struggling to breathe. Her colour isn't good."

The radio clicked. "Abby, are you there? You want us to return to town?"

"No, I'll handle it as first responder. I'll take her in the paddy wagon." She rung off. "Roman, we'll need some blankets to cushion her from the floor and keep her warm. Let's move."

Three minutes later, she had Edwina secured in the rear of the wagon, Warren and Roman kneeling either side. Abby closed the rear doors and hurried to take the wheel.

Lou caught her by the arm. "I'll follow as soon as I grab the twins, and let Tessa and Dodge know what's happening."

"Okay." Abby looked over to the small group huddled on the verandah. "Maybe also call someone to keep an eye on her friends?"

"No need. They'll insist on coming to the hospital."

"See you there then." Abby started the engine, flicked on her lights and siren and peeled down the drive and onto the road.

Her palms were damp as she gripped the steering wheel, hoping she'd make it in time. The old lady was well-liked and quite a figurehead in the small community.

It didn't take long to drive to the newly renovated Bindarra Creek Hospital. Once a small poly-clinic, the town had put the government grant money to good use with upgrades that now incorporated additional beds, X-ray and emergency departments.

Abby jolted to a stop at the front entrance and was out of the car the moment she turned off the engine. She opened the rear doors, then rushed to the reception area where she called for a wheelchair.

After hurrying back to the car, she assisted Roman and Warren in lifting Edwina into the chair.

Edwina's eyes snapped open and she clutched Abby's hand in a surprisingly strong grip. "Get Ty here. My solicitor. Must speak."

She sounded so insistent that Abby agreed to ferry the man to the hospital immediately.

The next few minutes were a blur of action and soon she was left standing in the waiting area with Roman. Warren had attempted to stay with Edwina but was waved back by the nurses. Through the wide glass double doors, Abby saw a group of people hurrying across the car park. Edwina's friends and family.

"I'll go and get Ty Devereaux. Want to come or do you prefer to wait?"

Roman took one look at the advancing crowd and shook his head. "I'll come with. Think she'll make it?"

"I have no idea, but she seems like a tough old bird."

They located Ty enjoying a morning stroll along the riverbank with his fiancé and it was only a matter of minutes before Abby and Roman with Ty stuffed in the rear of the paddy wagon, were back at the hospital. The waiting area was crowded with what looked like half the town milling about. Abby shot a keen glance around the room, noting Tessa and her child stood next to Warren and Lou. A hushed expectancy filled the air with tension, and Abby flexed her shoulders as she crossed to the ER reception.

A nurse approached, her glossy black hair neatly contained in a bun at the base of her neck. "May I help you, Constable?"

Deciding it wasn't necessary to correct the woman's assumption of her rank, Abby asked, "Any update on Ms Lette? I've brought her solicitor in at her request. I understood the matter to be urgent."

"Please wait while I check," the nurse responded in a soothing voice. She disappeared behind the security doors and reappeared moments later with a doctor new to town, a woman in her late twenties wearing a white coat over black trousers and sporting an amused glint in her eyes.

She held up her hands as the crowd surged to their feet. "Steady, everyone. No cause for alarm. Ms Lette is resting comfortably."

She turned to Warren and smiled. "It wasn't a heart attack. She's suffering from severe reflux which could be caused by a number of factors. I'll organise tests to check for a hiatal hernia and for food intolerances. It's also a possibility her symptoms were caused by eating foods with too high fat content."

"I knew it!" declared Pamela, lifting her chin in a pugnacious manner. "Didn't I tell her, Warren, to cut down on cake?"

Warren huffed out a relieved breath, his shoulders sagging. He sent a wry smile towards the solicitor. "Sorry about that, mate. Hope we didn't drag you away from anything important."

"Not a problem. I'll call back at visiting hours and check with Ms Lette to see whether she wants me to do anything for her." Smiling, Ty pushed up his sleeve and checked his watch. "Any chance of a lift, officer?"

"Hell. Thanks, Abby. You're a real trooper and we're bloody glad you're in our town," Warren interrupted. He wrung Abby's hand before bounding after the doctor and asking to see his mother-in-law.

"Sure. I'll drop you off at your office." Nodding to the solicitor, Abby led the way from the hospital as voices rose in an excited babble.

Roman caught her hand in his as they pushed through the doors. "Is it like this every day?"

"Pretty much." She tossed him a grin. "Welcome to life in a small town."

CHAPTER 7

This must be my lucky day. Roman forked over the cash before helping the owner of the Riverside Pub, who'd introduced himself as Dan, wrangle the bunk bed frames onto a box trailer. They rammed in two mattresses then covered the lot with a blue plastic tarp.

Roman bent over to hook one end of the jockey strap through the side rail before tossing the stretchy rope to the other side.

"These should do the trick." Dan gave the tarp one last tug before wiping his dusty hands together. "Hope you're going to make Bindarra your home. It's a good place to bring up kids."

A slow burn crept up the back of Roman's neck as he mumbled, "People seem friendly."

Dan laughed and crossed over to tie the tarp down on the other side of the trailer. "Nosy, you mean. Don't worry, mate. You'll get used to it. Check out the local IGA store. They usually have sheets, pillows, that kind of thing."

"I will. Cheers." Roman straightened, casting a glance around the rear yard of the pub. His eyes widened as he spotted a fishing kayak resting against the shed. "Get a lot of use out of your kayak?"

Dan shrugged. "Not as much as I'd like. Got a pub and gym to run these days." He scratched his chin in a reflective manner. "Tell you what. I've got a coupla kayaks some bloke left here a while back. Couldn't pay his bill, so he handed over some of his gear in exchange. I was thinking of advertising them for sale in the *Bindarra Bugle*. But, if you're interested…?"

"I'll definitely check them out."

"Awesome. Got them stashed around the back of the gym." Dan led the way to the back of the large shed which housed the gym, where they stopped and surveyed the two kayaks. "Both two-seaters. Is this what you're after?"

Roman let out a satisfied sigh. "Perfect. How much do you want for them?"

After a little bit of friendly haggling, Roman paid up then they placed the kayaks and paddles on top of the beds and mattresses and secured the lot with another couple of jockey straps.

Dan stood back and laughed. "Got quite a haul there, mate. Reckon the missus will have your guts for garters when she discovers your spending spree."

"Maybe, but the boys will love them. We'll test them out this weekend - if it doesn't rain and this blasted wind lets up." Casting a glance at the cloud covered sky, Roman tamped down his twinge of misgiving.

How *would* Abby react? And what the hell did he think he was doing? Acting like this was his family. Anticipating fun days on the water with a pair of homeless boys and his almost ex-wife.

It was only one day. Or was it?

I thought I was out of here as soon as possible. Now I'm day dreaming of a future that will never be mine.

Shaking off his unease, Roman shook Dan's hand and climbed behind the steering wheel.

Dan called out, "Don't forget my gym's open every day until ten at night, if you ever want a good workout. And we've got a boxing ring starting up."

"Yeah? I've done a bit of boxing in my day."

"Give me a call and we can set something up."

"I'll keep it in mind. Thanks Dan." A friendly wave of the hand, then Roman was off, driving along Main Street until he located the IGA supermarket. He found a double space in the carpark next door before striding to the front entrance of the store. An elderly Japanese guy and his equally elderly Caucasian wife strolled past, hand in hand, their faces bent toward each other, their expressions intent and filled with a love that caused Roman's chest to tighten unbearably.

He stalked through the plastic fly strips. There'd been a point in his life when he'd believed that could have been him and Abby one day in the far future. But not any longer. The reality was their life journeys no longer aligned. And it was time, he remembered he'd soon return to the Philippines.

Alone.

Feeling a little savage and more disappointed than he cared to admit, he marched down the aisles gathering pillows, sheets, and blankets into the trolley. Next, he turned his attention to replenishing the empty shelves in Abby's kitchen.

Focus on the task at hand. Then move on.

CHAPTER 8

Around mid-afternoon, Roman had the beds assembled in Abby's spare bedroom and the shelves and refrigerator stocked with food. He'd even found a couple of bean bags, one bright blue and the other orange, in the IGA store. The squishy bags now resided on the thread-bare carpet of the boys' room.

A series of beeps indicated the washing machine had finished its cycle and with Pinky prancing at his heels, he went to the laundry. He transferred the new linen from the washing machine to the line strung up along the rear verandah. The fierce wind should remove most of the moisture then after a short spin in the dryer, he'd be able to finish making up the beds.

Listen to me. I sound so domesticated.

He snorted. The little dog jumped up against his leg, clearly thinking he wanted to play. He scooped her up and gently fondled her tiny ears. He placed her on the ground, then went inside the house. After the dog followed,

Roman closed the thick, wooden door against the chill of the wind.

He'd been busy, and he felt a deep satisfaction with his achievements.

He'd lugged home a trailer-load of cut timber for the fireplace, dealt with the beds, and stacked the kayaks with their paddles, on the front verandah. From the oven, came the tantalising aroma of a slow-baked casserole.

At least the boys and Abby will have a decent meal tonight.

She'd never been much of a cook, preferring to leave that aspect of their wedded life to him. But when he gave it serious thought, he realised there were more nights when he'd been absent overseas for his job, than at home cooking dinner.

He replenished the little dog's water bowl before pulling on his windcheater and leaving the house. He'd return the box trailer to the garage where he'd hired it then come back to deal with the washing. Afterwards he'd pick up the boys from where they'd been told to wait at the police station once school had finished. Abby's shift wouldn't end until around six. Far too long to have a couple of teenagers cooped up inside. Kicking a football and running around the paddock for an hour should burn off a lot of their energy.

He started the car and drove down the pot-holed track and over the cattle grid, where he stopped. His blood cooled in his veins as the hairs on his arms bristled.

A convertible drove slowly past.

A dark-blue Lexus.

The car gathered speed then disappeared down the road.

❧

Dinner that night was a stark contrast to the previous.

After seeing the strange car, Roman knew he needed to have another serious discussion with Abby. And with the boys around, that meant after they'd gone to bed.

The wind whistled around the house. The warmth from the fire blazing in the lounge room had penetrated the kitchen where they sat at the dining table.

And, even more miraculous, Drew appeared more relaxed than he'd been earlier that day, the surly twist to his lips not visible for the moment.

Roman pretended not to notice as Eddie slipped Pinky, sitting ears pricked beside his chair, a small portion of tender braised steak from his plate.

"What's the go with the kayaks?" Abby popped a piece of herbed bread into her mouth, her green eyes dancing with amusement.

Roman shrugged. "What can I say? I couldn't resist. Dan reckons there're a few good spots in the Akuna National Park with easy launching into the river."

Abby's amusement vanished. "What about the rapids?"

"Only in two places and with the map I bought, we'll be able to avoid those sections. I thought if the wind eased and the rain held off, we could take a trip up there on Sunday." He paused before adding the clincher, "Got life jackets from the hardware shop."

"Hope you didn't buy me one. I still have my own." Abby dabbed at her lips with the napkin.

"I didn't know you'd kept your kayak." His mind filled with memories of kayaking with Abby when on holidays in New Zealand and Tasmania. "How long since you've been on the water?"

Abby grimaced wryly. "Too long - which means my muscles will tell me quite loudly on Monday just how long it's been. If we go that is."

Roman laughed. "It'll do you good."

Drew placed his fork onto the table, his gaze darting to Roman first then settling on Abby.

Smart kid. Already knows who's the real boss here.

Roman took a sip of water from his glass and waited.

"We're really going kayaking." Drew sucked in a sharp breath. "What? All of us?"

"Yes. All of us." Abby pushed a strand of hair behind her ears. "Don't get too excited. It'll depend on the weather. And there is no negotiation over wearing life jackets."

"Choice!" Drew sucked in a breath while Eddie looked fit to burst with excitement. "We haven't done anything like that before. Is it hard?"

Roman shook his head. "These are touring kayaks which means easy paddling over quiet water. Now, white water rafting that is totally different." He had to choke back the words forming on his lips ... *I'll teach you someday* ... Passing a hand over his face, he remained silent.

"That's totally mag." Drew's eyes shone.

Eddie pushed back his chair and dashed to the kitchen window, shoved back the curtain, and peered into the night. "What if it rains?"

He sounded so anxious that Roman found himself reassuring the kid, "Not a problem. There's always the weekend after."

He felt the impact of Abby's surprised stare.

"Yay!" Eddie shouted and, a big grin on his face, ran back to drop into his chair.

Pinky yapped hysterically.

But it was the shy smile on Drew's face that just about did Roman in, the kid looked dazed, as if unable to believe he was feeling happy.

Bloody hell. I'm getting involved.

CHAPTER 9

"Where are you going with this, Roman?" Abby sank back into the couch and blew on her hot tea. "Forking out for kayaks, for heaven's sake."

Roman lifted his shoulders, a helpless expression on his face. "I honestly don't know."

Abby sighed. She suspected she knew what was going on. He'd been caught up in the moment. Carried away by an idea, a fantasy, the dream they'd both yearned for, for so many years.

A family of their own.

The house was quiet, the two boys, amazingly, entrenched in their room doing homework. And after a single grumble.

Roman hadn't been the only one caught up in a make-believe moment. While the boys and Roman had kicked a ball around the paddock, she'd left work early and hunted out a thick magenta rug and the matching magenta, thermal curtains she'd packed away on top of her wardrobe. Left-overs from her former life.

It had only taken fifteen minutes to spread the rug on the boys' bedroom floor and hang the curtains over the thin roller blind covering the window giving the room a cheerful, homely feel. Even better, the curtains were sufficiently heavy to muffle the chill from the glass and the cold air that seeped through the cracks in the badly fitted pane.

Abby sighed inwardly, thinking about when the boys had walked into the bedroom and saw the beds cosily made up with doonas and plump pillows, the brightly coloured bean bags, the cheerful rug and new curtains.

Eddie had dashed straight inside and dived on the bean bag with a cheerful yell. Drew, as Abby had expected, had hung back, all quiet and serious-like as he'd mumbled a quiet, *"thank you"* before claiming the top bunk.

Even now, her eyes burned at the memory.

Since then, Drew had been quiet all evening, like he was pondering some tricky question inside his head. Eddie had been like a fire cracker, energy sizzling from every pore, and couldn't stop talking once he'd learned about the possibility of kayaking this coming weekend. All through dinner. All through the game of Monopoly they'd played afterwards.

Satisfaction sat deep in Abby's soul. Taking the boys in, had been the right thing to do. And the way Roman had slipped so easily into their old routine of shared domestic chores filled her with comfort.

But it's only for a few weeks. Then they'll be gone.

Abby shivered, shutting down the insidious reminder.

The dying fire hissed a spurt of steam, making Pinky

jump. She trotted from her dog bed, and leapt onto the chaise to settle in Abby's lap.

Absently, Abby stroked her with one hand.

"Want me to take that?" Roman indicated her mug.

Abby nodded. "It's too hot anyway."

Roman placed the mug onto the coffee table then settled back with his small shot of whiskey and took a sip.

Maybe it would be better not to delve too deep into the why behind both their actions today. Maybe it would be better to focus on the moment instead. Relaxing against the soft cushions on her back, Abby asked, "What about your job?"

"I've taken long service leave and some unpaid leave. I've left my return date open."

Her eyebrows rose. "Seriously? That doesn't sound like you." Her voice turned hard.

He sat up abruptly and turned to her. "Look. I made mistakes. We both made mistakes, Abby." He compressed his mouth for a few seconds before adding, "I've been thinking about retiring."

"What? *You?* I thought you loved that job." She bit back the words...*more than me, more than our desire for a baby*. It was an old argument that made her tired thinking about.

"I do. Or rather I did love it. But it's more a young person's game and I'm getting on." He gave a quick smile. "I'm forty-three this year."

"That's not old and you've got plenty of good years left," Abby said softly, thinking of her own fast-approaching birthday.

"Thanks, hon. But after fifteen years of specialist military service followed by ten years rescuing people in insane terrain, my body isn't what it used to be."

Sternly repressing her impulse to ogle said body, she pointed out, "You don't have to be on the field. You could take a desk job. I'm certain the company would hate to lose your expertise."

He nodded. "They've made that offer. I turned it down. Truth is, Abby. I want to do something else with my life, something where I can sleep at night." He frowned into his shot glass. "The memories haunt me. The faces, the twisted bodies, the grief, the fear, the desperation, it's there every time I close my eyes. I've been doing art therapy for two years now. It helps. And I've discovered I like it."

Abby took his hand in hers and gripped it tight. His skin was familiar and yet different beneath her touch. The desire to re-discover everything about him began to grow inside her heart. A little shaken, she gently released her hold. "What will you do?"

"I've got some ideas."

"A budding Picasso?" she teased.

He grinned. "You never know."

As the shadows faded from his eyes, delight coursed through her, and she laughed.

He set his glass down onto the coffee table. "I thought about moving back to Australia. Settling down."

Abby jerked her hand from his. "So, this is where you tell me, you've met someone." The words came out harsher than she'd intended, and she winced inwardly. It would never do, to show how much that notion held the power to hurt. Like a knife plunged deep into her heart.

"Huh?" He turned startled eyes toward her. "Hell, no, Abby." A sheepish expression crossed his face. "I did date a couple of women a few times."

"I'd have been surprised if you hadn't," Abby said. Who wouldn't want to hook a man of his integrity? Roman had always been the kind of guy who turned heads, the moment he walked into a room. Men wanted to be like him, envying his quiet self-assurance and easy air of command. Women wanted to drag him off to their beds and into their lives.

"What about you? I can't imagine blokes not pounding on your door to ask you out."

"I've dated a few times." *But none of them were you.* And settling for second best wasn't fair on anyone.

"This looks like a good town," Roman said slowly.

"You don't mean … you aren't seriously considering living here?" Her voice rose to a squeak.

"Why not? I already know the local cop and met quite a lot of people in the course of one day." He grinned but his eyes remained steady, serious, considering, as they fixed on hers.

Heat flushed through her body. She curled her short-cut nails into her palms and fought the urge to scream *"Yes!"*.

Then the memories flooded her.

How could she bear seeing him day by day living a life separate from her own? It would be too much of a poignant reminder of all they'd lost. Even after five long years, the bitterness that had withered their rapport still dominated her heart. She refused to let go of the past. She couldn't.

She snapped, "I don't think that's a good idea. We have too much history."

"It was only an idea," he muttered. After reaching for his glass, Roman tossed the whiskey down his throat. He settled it back down with a thud of finality. "I saw that Lexus, Elizabeth spoke about."

"Really? When? Where?"

"This afternoon, driving along the road out front about three-fifteen."

"Holy smokes! What if Elizabeth was right? Any chance you got the rego number?"

Roman shook his head, face grim. "Couldn't see it. The plates were covered with mud."

"Coincidence or deliberate?"

"Hard to say. There was mud all over the rear of the car and the side I could see."

"Damn. Okay, I'll ask around town tomorrow."

"Thought you were going to do that today?"

Abby shrugged sheepishly. "I didn't feel there was any credence in Elizabeth's statement. Plus, it's been a busy day. But if you've seen the car cruising about town, that makes her fears more real. I'll start digging first thing tomorrow."

She turned a serious face towards Roman. "You know what this means, don't you?"

He nodded. "The kids could well be in danger."

"No way will I send them back until I'm certain they'll be safe."

He squeezed her hand. "How long do the foster papers cover you for again?"

Frowning over the sharp, lonely pang that twisted her heartstrings, Abby said slowly, "Four weeks."

"That's not very long."

"We'll have to work fast."

"I'll keep an eye out and let you know the second I see that bloody car."

"Thanks." Blinking away the stupid surge of happiness, she said slowly, "I wonder what kind of danger the boys are in. Do you think it's something to do with their parents? Remember, it was their mother who emphasised she needed the boys protected."

"True. It's possible the parents or either one of them were involved in some kind of criminal activity."

"But why come after the kids? Unless, it's something they've heard or seen?"

"We could question them but that won't be easy. Especially if we start probing about their dead mother."

Pinky yawned and jumped off Abby's lap to settle in her basket. Frowning, Abby picked up her luke-warm tea and took a sip. "Let's keep it low-key for the moment. I can do a discrete name search through the police database. See if anything pops."

"I like that approach. No point in upsetting the boys if we don't have to."

"Agreed." Abby fell silent while Roman stared into the flames.

She wondered what he was thinking and whether he was remembering their previous life together. How did he feel being back in her presence? He'd given no indication he was resentful of being pulled away from his life overseas. In fact, so far, he'd given the impression of a man quite content doing chores and spending time with her and two homeless boys.

I could ask.

Heart racing, Abby squelched the thought. If she asked him how he felt, he'd want to know how she felt. And she had no intention of admitting how much the thought of his presence filled her with joy, joy and anguish in equal measure.

Truth be told, she didn't know what to make of her emotions.

After a few minutes, she cleared her throat delicately. "I did source some school clothes for the boys, so they won't feel the odd ones out. If you're dropping the boys off at school tomorrow, can you please attend the office? There should be a parcel set aside with my name."

Roman took her lead. "I'm all over it. Do they need any other clothes?"

Abby shook her head. "No. I've already got them three long-sleeve blue polo shirts and a grey school jumper each. They're allowed to wear whatever coats or jackets they like in winter. And some of the kids wear jeans not the regulation grey trousers."

Roman looked over at her. "That accident your work mates attended? Was it … serious?"

"Serious enough. No fatalities but one person had to be taken to hospital with a suspected broken leg. The other four were treated on the scene. Loads of paperwork for us, though. Then, blow me down, if we didn't get another phone call from Pastor Miller when I was about to clock off." Abby sighed then told Roman about the reverend's previous calls and lack of any evidence at the church. "Tomorrow, I'll hunt down his wife and have a chat."

"Heard anything about Edwina?"

Abby grinned. "She's doing fine and demanding to be released from hospital. Apparently, the doctor caught her heading out the front door, her IV drip trailing behind her, and ordered her back to bed. I think she'll be going home tomorrow." She wagged a finger at him. "About those kayaks …"

"Can't back out now. We're both committed. Our names will be dirt if we renege."

"I feel like I've been out-manoeuvred somehow," Abby muttered.

Roman laughed and nudged her with his shoulder. "Hon, no one can out-manoeuvre you."

"And don't you forget it." Abby laughed.

CHAPTER 10

The following morning found Roman browsing The Phoenix – Restoration & Repair Antiques shop located on Main Street. With interest, he picked up an ornate, black mantle clock, turning it slowly over in his hands. Judging by the weight, it was solid marble. The clock had three arches, the centre and largest arch was the exact width of the brass face, which was dull and mottled, in need of a good clean. He peered closer. The brass hands failed to move. He listened. No ticking.

"Sorry, mate. It's not for sale," came a voice from behind him.

Roman glanced up and saw a younger guy about thirty years of age with short, brown hair, sporting an old-fashioned carpenter's belt around his hips. The steadiness of his cool gaze reminded Roman of Abby. This, then, must be the copper whose job Abby had taken when the guy had resigned a few years ago. "It's Victorian vintage, isn't it? Eight-day movement?"

"Yeah. You know your stuff." The bloke moved closer,

indicating with his forefinger without touching the clock. "See this pink marble around the black base and the top of the two plinths bracketing the face? Very unusual for its time period."

"It's a beauty." Roman held his breath, feeling almost reverent at the piece of history he held in his hands. "Are you keeping it for yourself?"

The owner shook his head. "No way, mate. It doesn't work."

"That's not a problem for me. I'm willing to give it a go. My grandfather was a clock maker."

"Nice." The other guy thought for a moment. "I guess I could sell, as long as you take it as is. I'm Dodge Myers, by the way."

"Roman Taylor." Roman juggled the clock under his arm and extended his hand.

Dodge glanced down, pausing a beat, before giving a firm shake. "Heard from my wife and Gran, you're not related to that bastard who hurt my family."

"Only through an unfortunate marriage." Roman quirked his eyebrows. "Ms Lette is your grandmother? How is she today?"

Dodge grinned. "At home and raising a hell of a commotion. She's got Dad, Lou and Tessa running around, fetching and carrying. Glad I'm at work and out of the firing line."

"This all yours?" Roman jerked his chin sideways.

"Yep. Been away for a few days and just got back from an auction out Warrego way. Caught myself a few bargains." Dodge rocked back on his heels, slipped his thumbs into his belt and narrowed his eyes.

Classic cop stance.

Roman stifled his smile as he recalled the number of occasions he'd seen Abby enact the same position. Must have been something they learnt at training.

"Understand you're staying at the house," Dodge said.

"Yes. I'm uncertain how long I'll be in town."

"Then we'll be seeing a lot of each other."

Roman grinned. "Don't worry. Even if I can't get the clock working again, I've got no intention of whinging or demanding my money back."

"Good to know. Alright then, let me crunch some numbers." Dodge edged his way along the crowded aisle to the front counter where, after scribbling figures on a pad, he came up with a price that Roman accepted without a quibble.

He wanted that clock.

He could see it squatting, solid, splendid and glorious on a timber mantle above a stone fire-place. In the background, he imagined people seated on a couch in front of the flames. Abby, those two boys …

With a start, Roman shook his head and came back to reality.

Dodge eyed him curiously. "You alright, mate? You look like you've seen a ghost."

"Speaking of which, I understand you've got a resident ghost yourself?"

Dodge laughed. "Gran swears by her." He tapped a thoughtful finger on the counter. "The thing is, both Tessa and Kaylee reckon they've seen her too."

"Stranger things have been known to happen." Roman grinned.

"Don't tell me you're another believer!"

"Just saying." Roman spread his hands. "Had a strange

experience in a Columbian mine a few years back. There'd been a tunnel collapse, and the trapped miners had tried to find another way out and became disorientated. I was leading a small rescue team, and I swear to this day, I heard the voice of a young kid calling me. I followed the sound and we ended up finding the miners. But there were no children amongst them. I've got no rational explanation for what happened."

"You don't say?" Dodge pulled a box made from thick cardboard out from under the counter.

"You sound like my wife. She doesn't believe in the paranormal either." Roman watched while Dodge placed the clock inside the box, then packed handfuls of shredded paper around the sides.

"Hear you're interested in boxing?" Dodge asked as he stuck down the lid with sticky-tape.

Small towns. Unbelievable. "All I said to Dan, the owner - I think of the Riverside pub? Was that I've done some boxing in my day."

Dodge grinned. "Doesn't take much here and we'll have you roped into whatever activity where we need bodies. Another trainer would be good to help out on school sport days. We're hoping to start up another class for teenagers. Keep them busy and out of trouble."

"I'm only passing through."

"Dunno about that." Dodge scratched his chin. "What did you say you did for a living?"

"I didn't but I'm part of a global rescue team. We've got bases all around the world. I currently work out of Manila."

"Sounds like you're exactly the person we need."

"Huh?" Roman eyed the younger bloke warily. If he

wasn't careful, he'd be sucked into this community and welded in tighter than a can of sardines.

"Our current SES captain has retired and already left the district. We could do with someone with your experience to take over his role."

"I'm only here a few days …" Roman mumbled while already, his mind teemed with ideas and his body fizzed at the prospect of a new challenge.

And an excuse to stay.

"Think about it, mate. In the meantime, why not drop by the station and check us out? We've got a meeting tomorrow night to discuss the vacant captain's position. We usually train every Tuesday at six thirty. Bring those boys of yours. Seven p.m. sharp. Your wife should be there if she isn't on duty." Dodge winked.

Roman found himself nodding and not bothering to explain his relationship to Drew and Eddie. Or his soon-to-be-over marriage. Exasperated over his easy capitulation, he rubbed a hand over his forehead and glared out the doorway.

He stiffened.

Beside him, Dodge let out a surprised gasp.

Roman bounded towards the door.

Dodge moved with him.

They collided, wedged together in the doorway until with muffled curses they both wiggled sideways and burst through like popping corks to emerge on the footpath.

Roman paced to the side of the road and stared down the street. *Damn.* No sign of that car now. Shaking his head, he went back to the shop where the other bloke soon joined him.

"What did you see?" Dodge asked in a curious voice.

"A car I've been trying to track down. What about you?"

"A former partner coming out of the shop across the road. But I must have been mistaken. Sara is in prison."

Roman sent him a startled glance.

"Long story."

"So's mine." Now that was a strange coincidence. A mysterious car, the boys needing protection from who-knew-what, and Dodge thinking he saw someone who should be in prison. Could it all be connected?

Roman picked up the box and made a decision. "See you tomorrow night."

CHAPTER 11

Cemeteries were desolate places at the best of times and even more dismal when visiting in the middle of a raw winter when the weak sun was playing hide and seek behind thick grey clouds. Abby dug her stiff hands deeper into the pockets of her police-issue jacket and shivered as a particularly icy blast of wind whipped across her face, making her eyes water. She sent her companion an encouraging smile as he continued his monologue on Bindarra Creek's history as they strolled among the gravestones.

"And this is the grave of Peter Lette, died in 1886. Came over from Ireland with his wife, Anne, in 1856. They had a farm of forty acres to the south of town where they grew crops and after three miscarriages, had two children. The daughter, Rose, drowned in their dam. Bless her soul." Reverend Miller shook his head sadly. "The Lettes purchased an acre of land in town and their son, Doran, built Fig Tree Lodge in 1889. There's been Lettes living there ever since."

Chest puffing with pride, Reverend Miller gestured to the red-brick building behind him and continued, "St Ignatius was a mere wattle and daub hut back in 1861. This building was built in 1882 from locally sourced bricks on the site of the original church. There wasn't much here in Bindarra in those days. It started out as a staging post for bullock teams taking people from Armidale to Moree, but we soon thrived. We had a store, three public houses, one of which was burnt to the ground in 1902. What a night that was! A school, and two working gold mines that brought money and people to town."

Abby listened with interest. History had always fascinated her, from a distance. Personally, the thought of no running hot-water, hours of back-breaking work from sun-up to sun-down held zero appeal to her.

But the reverend spoke as if he'd lived in those far-flung days, his voice melodic and sounding full of memories as he brought the past alive with his words.

Abby narrowed her eyes.

His expression was dreamy, and his mind fixed in the past.

Maybe too much in the past.

"There were several large grazing properties and we had free settlers as well as convicts. It's said Thunderbolt used to visit this area. The thief even had the audacity to step foot inside my church! But I'll show him. I'll show all those thieves. The sinners shall not go unpunished."

Abby shot a sharp glance at him then cleared her throat. "Are you talking about the bushranger?"

Or are you talking about the prowler you thought you saw the other night?

She frowned, not liking the vengeful ring in the reverend's normally tranquil tone.

"Of course I am. Are you deaf? How I wish I'd been alive in those days. I would have taught him the meaning of the word, 'respect'."

"Mmmm," Abby responded noncommittally and decided not to point out that Thunderbolt had been dead and buried a good twelve years before the current version of St Ignatius was built.

Worried, she attempted to drag the good pastor back to the present. "Now, Reverend, can you please tell me again what happened the night before last."

He huffed out an irritated breath. "I've already given my statement. You were there!"

"I know, sir, but sometimes going over the same events causes a new memory to spring to life."

"Very well. I'll show you." Without glancing in her direction, he clomped off in his gumboots.

Shoulders hunched against the bite of the westerly wind, Abby followed until they reached the church. She took a moment to admire the intricacy and rich colours of the recently restored pointed arch motif with timber tracery windows and the symmetrical façade of the Old Colonial Gothic style building with its tall tower and battlement parapet. She could see why Reverend Miller was determined to preserve the building.

The reverend stopped and appeared to have fallen into a state of wordless wonder as he stared dead ahead.

The seconds ticked on until she promoted "Reverend Miller?"

The seconds ticked on. Abby followed his gaze.

Nothing but red bricks met her eyes. She prompted, "Sir, you were telling me about the attempted break-in."

"What?" He turned to face her, blinking madly, his eyes looking unfocused. "Who are you? What am I doing here?"

Uh, oh.

Abby said softly, "I'm a friend. Abby Taylor. Come with me. I'll take you home." She gently cupped her hand over his elbow and led the reverend back to the vicarage where she knocked on the door.

"Is that you, Jonas?" Florrie Miller's voice floated down the hall.

The reverend toed off his gumboots then opened the screen door. He ambled towards the kitchen, seemingly oblivious to Abby following behind. Rubbing his hands together, he beamed around the kitchen. "Is that a pot of tea?"

"Yes, dear. And your favourite. Fresh scones, whipped cream and a pot of Beatrix's famous, home-made blackberry jam." Florrie pushed her husband gently into a chair then looked at Abby. She didn't seem surprised to see a policewoman in her home but perhaps as a vicar's wife, she was used to people coming and going. "I'll set another plate for you, Senior Constable. Sit down, please."

Thinking about her waistline and how difficult she was finding it to keep the weight off her hips lately, Abby was about to refuse until Florrie placed a plate of scones, direct from the oven, onto the table. Surely one little scone couldn't hurt? Abby drew out a chair and sat. "Thank you, Mrs Miller."

The elderly woman waved a hand. "Oh please. Florrie

will do just fine." She trotted to the back door and poking her head outside, called, "Cooee! Tea's up!"

Moving back to the counter, she picked up the teapot and brought it over to the table, explaining, "Edwina and Pam are collecting the eggs from our coop. They'll join us in a minute."

So much for a quiet word alone with the pastor's wife. The woman was harder to pin down than a butterfly. But if Abby hurried, she may get a few answers before the other ladies came back to the house. "Mrs Miller, I mean Florrie, did you hear any noises or see anyone lurking around the church?"

"Those nights when Jonas called the station?"

Upon Abby's nod, Florrie picked up a mug and cradled it while she thought. "No. Can't say that I did. The first I knew there was something wrong was when Jonas marched into the bedroom and asked where we'd put the rifle."

Rifle? Holy ...! Choosing her words with care, Abby said, "I don't believe you mentioned anything about a gun in your previous statements."

"Oh, didn't I, dear? Is this an official visit?" Florrie sent Abby a keen glance then popped the mug onto the table. "Never mind. I only remembered Jonas doing that now when you asked. The gun is mine, and I've got a license."

Abby's head reeled. She just couldn't picture this kind, placid woman in a hunting outfit, squinting down the barrel of a rifle aimed at some hapless joey.

Abby placed a scone onto her plate and reached for the butter dish. "What's the rifle used for?"

"It's no secret. The whole town knows I'm a fully paid-up member of the Sporting Shooters Association of Australia."

Struck dumb, Abby couldn't think of a word to say.

Florrie chuckled and moved closer to pat Abby's shoulder. "Don't look so horrified, dear. Target shooting only. I could never kill a living creature."

The back door opened and in trooped her cronies, Edwina Lette and then Pamela Brown, who carried a basket of eggs in front of her like an offering to the gods.

Edwina winked at Abby and bore no resemblance to the grey-faced old woman she'd last seen being wheeled into hospital. "I've escaped. Blasted family. Wanting me to stay in bed all day. Nothing wrong with my ticker so I didn't see no reason to waste a perfectly good day lying about."

"I'm keeping an eye on her," said Pamela gruffly while Edwina snorted. "Good layers, you've got there, Florrie."

"I've got four young hens that should start laying this spring, if you'd like them, Pam?"

"Thanks, Florrie. We've got enough chooks of our own." Pamela Brown nodded at Abby, then smiled at the reverend while she popped the basket of eggs onto the sink. "Enjoyed your sermon last Sunday, Jonas."

Edwina piped up as she drew out a chair, "Can't say that I did, all that yakking about God's vengeance. Put me off my sausages and fried eggs."

Abby noticed the old lady refrained from adding cream or butter to her scone, merely spreading a thin layer of jam over the top. It seemed her recent bout in hospital may have changed her eating habits for the good.

Pamela stiffened. "If you're going to be so critical, I don't know why you bothered to turn up."

"You and me both, Pam. But Matilda told me I needed to be there."

"Honestly, Edwina. I wish you'd stop talking about your long-dead relative as if she was here with us today."

"You should open your mind to new experiences, Pam. Now, take poor Roy. When are you going to put him out of his misery?"

"Mind your own business!"

"The scones are getting cold," Florrie intervened.

The two old ladies bristled at each other over the brims of their tea cups.

"Ignore them, dear. They're the best of friends." Florrie sat beside her husband and poured him out a cup of tea. "Have a scone, darling." She pushed the bowl of whipped cream towards Jonas who, looking a little confused, began to spoon the cream onto his plate.

Florrie briskly took over, spreading jam then popping some cream onto the scone and pushing the plate a little closer to her husband.

Jonas took a bite and Florrie sighed.

"Actually, I wouldn't mind some chooks," Abby surprised herself by saying.

Florrie looked over and smiled. "No worries, dear. Send that lovely man of yours over anytime to collect them." She turned to her friends. "I was telling Abby about our little shooting group."

Edwina popped an entire scone into her mouth and mumbled through bulging cheeks, "Florrie's the best shooter out of the lot of us."

Florrie blushed.

After a long five seconds examining the reverend's

wife, Abby turned and eyed the elderly woman with the devilish twinkle in her eyes. "You're also a member?"

Now, that I can believe.

"Yep." Edwina dusted crumbs off her hands before wiping her mouth with a yellow napkin liberally decorated with red poppies. She tossed the crumpled linen onto the table. "We all are, me, Florrie here, Pam, Beatrix, Kathleen Sullivan, have you met her yet?"

Abby shook her head.

"Nice woman. You'll get on with her like a house on fire. She's like you, a woman who can get things done."

And she isn't the only one.

Abby held back her mirth.

Edwina continued to tick people's names off her fingers. "There's also Mary Moonie who runs that dusty old museum of hers, and Esther Ainslie. Wish she wouldn't insist on bringing her damn Poodle to our meets. The noise only makes the poor thing go crazy barking. We're the Bindarra Creek Women's Target Rifle Shooting Club and I tell you, we're good. Won the State and Nationals a few times. Reckon we're good enough for the Olympics."

Pamela snorted. "What? At our age?"

"Never too late to try new things." Edwina smirked then winked.

Making sucking noises, Pamela audibly ground her false teeth.

Abby stirred the milk in her tea and wondered how on earth the conversation had gone so completely off-track.

The reverend leaned back against his chair, folded his arms over his small pot belly, and closed his eyes. A soft snore escaped. Obviously, he was able to tune out after years of listening to his wife's friends' crazy conversations.

Taking a loud slurp of her tea, Edwina fixed her gimlet stare onto Abby. "We could do with some younger blood in our club. What do you say, Abby? Care to join?"

"I'll think about it." Inwardly, she shuddered at the thought of spending hours in these ladies' company. Honestly? They scared the hell out of her. One whiff of her precarious marital state, and she had a suspicion they'd be ruthless in their pursuit of changing it for what they believed would be the better.

She was happy with her choice of a life lived alone.

Wasn't she?

"But you were asking about our prowler." Florrie dabbed her mouth delicately with the napkin before placing it neatly on the table and folding her hands over the top of it. "Those nights when you came out to investigate, I'm sorry to say that I heard nothing. I didn't see anything either. However, when I was returning from the CWA hall last Friday around six-thirty p.m., I'm certain there was someone walking about the cemetery."

"Not another ghost," groaned Pamela, while Edwina perked up visibly.

"No, dear. This was someone quite different. A real person." Florrie's brow wrinkled. "I had a feeling I'd seen them before."

Abby wondered whether she should whip out her notebook. "Just the one person? Male or female?"

"One person and I can't say whether it was a man or woman. I'm sorry. It was a dark night and I was some distance away. I suppose it was the way they walked that I thought I'd recognised. But it's so hard to tell who anyone is in winter what with the coats and beanies we all wear."

"Then the person was wearing a coat and a beanie?" Abby probed.

"Why, yes! I do believe you're right. I did see something after all. It was one of those puffer jackets, you know, the type that makes us look twenty kilos heavier." Florrie beamed.

"Then what happened?"

Florrie looked surprised. "Nothing. I simply kept walking home."

"Did they notice you? Act strange or furtive?"

"Not really. They had their head bent and kept wandering about the cemetery. It could have been someone looking for a particular gravesite. There's no reason they were involved."

"I guess that's possible although if it was someone from town, they'd be able to head straight to the grave of their loved one." Abby tapped the table with her forefinger for a few seconds while the old ladies all watched her avidly. "I don't suppose you saw a strange car parked nearby? What about anyone new to town in the last couple of days?"

The three elderly women drew in noisy breaths, anticipation gleaming in their eyes.

"We've got this incredibly sexy man staying at the lodge." Edwina snickered.

Abby's cheeks burned.

"Be serious, Edwina. Can't you see the senior constable is on the job?" Nose quivering, Pamela looked across the table at Abby. "Anyone in particular we should keep an eye out for?"

"I'll get a pad and pencil." Florrie rose from her chair and opened a drawer. Returning to the table, she sat down again with pencil poised over a writing pad. "Go on. All of us are members of the Bindarra Creek Neighbourhood Watch Committee."

Of course, they are. I should have remembered that!

But it wouldn't hurt to have more eyes helping her out. "I'm interested in the whereabouts of a particular car and also, information about who the driver might be."

"This is so exciting," murmured Florrie as she scribbled on her pad.

Edwina grinned and clapped her hands, making the reverend start before he settled back down to his snooze. "We'll be undercover. Real James Bond stuff."

"I don't want anyone approaching this vehicle or its owner." Abby waited until the other women nodded in unison. "It's a dark blue or navy-blue Lexus convertible. I want to know where it goes, who the driver speaks to, and where the driver is staying in town. And a description of the driver would be helpful."

"You'll need the number plates." Florrie scribbled some more.

Heat crawled over her cheeks as Abby nodded. "Yes, of course."

"And that's it? That's all you want?" Edwina sounded disappointed.

"I think that is more than enough. And remember, do not approach the driver. If you see it, phone me on this number." Abby rattled off her personal mobile number which Florrie jotted down.

"We can take our rifles while we go on recon," said Edwina thoughtfully.

Oh. My. God!

"*No!*" Abby fought to calm herself. Really, what had she been thinking drafting these crazy but well-meaning crack pots into her plans? "No guns. If I find you on the streets carrying, I'll charge you and lock you up." She placed her hands palms down on the table and fixed the old women with a steely stare.

Edwina pouted. "*You* are no fun."

"That's because I'm the law."

I can't believe I just said that.

Abby kept her expression serious as Edwina muttered about her rights and Pamela Brown began to stack the dishes.

One more stern glare at each woman and Abby rose to her feet. "It's time I went. Thank you for the tea, Florrie."

"Anytime, dear. I'll walk you to the door."

Florrie followed her down the hall where Abby paused on the front porch.

"Mrs Miller, Florrie …," Abby hesitated a beat. "About your husband. He seems to be suffering from a level of confusion. When we were in the churchyard before coming inside the house, he didn't seem to know where he was and had appeared to have forgotten who I was."

Tears formed in Florrie's eyes, but she remained silent.

Abby ploughed on. "I wondered, well actually, both the senior sergeant and I wondered whether you'd noticed any changes in him lately."

"You want to know if my husband is going senile and invented the prowler." Florrie drew herself up straight. "Let me tell you, Senior Constable, Jonas may be getting on in years, but if he said he saw a person near the church, then take my word for it, someone *was* there."

"My apologies, Mrs Miller," Abby said, taking her cue from the other woman's switch to sudden formality. "I didn't mean to offend. Your husband is a wonderful man and I know the community thinks highly of him. Should anything else happen, please contact the station immediately."

One quick nod, then Florrie Miller stepped back and closed the door.

CHAPTER 12

While sipping his beer, Roman took a good look around the small bistro located in a room on the northern side of the Riverside Pub. The wide windows looked over the reserve that fell sharply down to the Akuna River. Being late afternoon, the sun had slipped over the horizon and darkness blacked what in daylight must be a spectacular view of the river and Kingfisher Bridge.

Roman looked across the table at Abby, admiring the way her short-sleeved, dark green dress hugged her curves and how brightly her blonde hair shone beneath the overhead lights. "Can't believe how warm it got this afternoon."

"Yes, it's very unusual for this time of year. Especially after that cold snap we've had all last month." Abby took a mouthful of her prawn linguine. When she finished chewing, she added, "It was freezing when I was at the cemetery this morning until the wind dropped and the clouds disappeared."

"Were there any ghosts?" mumbled Eddie.

Abby raised her eyebrows. "Don't speak with your mouth full."

Eddie nodded then swallowed.

Smiling, Abby said, "No ghosts. But I did learn a lot about Bindarra Creek's history."

"Sounds like being at school." Drew snorted and reached for his glass of Coke.

Abby laughed. "I guess it was a bit. Reverend Miller was very forthcoming."

"How was he today?" Roman remembered what Abby had told him regarding the reverend's recent behaviour.

"Quite sharp, then he became a little confused until I walked him to the rectory. He seemed to be fine then." Abby toyed with her fork before sending a searching glance at the two boys. She drew a breath as if she'd come to a decision. "A few members of the neighbourhood watch committee were also there, so I asked them to keep an eye out for the Lexus. Which reminds me Drew, Eddie."

She waited until they both looked up. "If you see a dark-blue convertible, let either Roman or myself know. And whatever you do, don't go near the car or the driver."

"Cool! Is he a robber?" Eddie, his eyes as round as saucers, popped a heaped forkful of spaghetti into his mouth.

"No, a person of interest."

"That's what the cops always say when they've got someone in their sights," Drew said and frowned.

"No cause to worry, mate. Simply, keep away from the car if you see it," Roman said in his best reassuring voice.

It must have worked because the anxiety lifted from the older boy's face and he smiled.

Roman met Abby's eyes. "I saw the car in town this morning but although I drove around the streets for an hour, I didn't spot it again. How did you get on?"

"Nothing on the police files. No reports of a stolen Lexus convertible and I can't put a KLO4 on the car until we've more to go on."

"Huh? What's a KLO4?" Drew paused, loaded fork inches from his mouth.

"Keep a look out for."

Drew grinned. "Choice. It's like being in a TF show."

"Without the car chases or guns blazing," Abby murmured.

"But that's the best part," said Drew.

Abby and Roman laughed.

Roman took another sip of his beer before placing it on the table. "How did school go?"

Drew hunched his shoulders. "Okay. It's kinda weird having the high school in the same yard as the little kids' school."

"Hey! I'm not a little kid!" Eddie scowled.

Ignoring Eddie's outburst, Abby said, "We're in the process of renovating the former high school building. At the moment, there are only a few demountables for the older students. The other building has been closed for a few years because the population fell too low to justify the maintenance. Not to mention teachers' salaries."

Roman grimaced. "Would have been hard keeping professionals and tradespeople in the town if the economy was dying."

Abby took a sip of her white wine before replying. "All

that was turned around though once the town managed to obtain a government grant. They put in a lot of initiatives that attracted people to the area. And now we've got a bigger hospital and will soon have a bigger school. But you're right, Roman. We need more people, more nurses and teachers, ones who will stay."

"Well, there's certainly a lot going for this town. I see a poster at the lodge after a scavenger challenge to attract tourists to the area. That sounds like fun." Roman grinned and raised his glass in a mock toast.

"We had the first one last year. It's part of our weeklong organic festival held in September. Lots of stalls with homemade goods and events featuring local artists and writers."

"Mmmm." Setting his beer down, Roman stroked his chin. "I could enter a few paintings in this year's event. Maybe go in the challenge. If I'm still here." He deliberately infused his voice with a taunting tone but although her cheeks flushed with sudden colour, his delightful wife failed to engage.

"Eddie, you've got spaghetti sauce on your chin." Head held high, Abby handed over a napkin.

"Thanks." Eddie wiped off the offending red stain and placed the crumpled napkin back onto the table before returning to his enjoyment of his meal.

"Looser." Smirking, Drew nudged his brother, causing Eddie to drop his fork on the floor.

Eddie pushed back, then shucked in an elbow dig for good measure.

"Okay, you two, settle down," ordered Abby.

Roman took the last bite of his pan-fried barramundi then wiped his mouth with a paper napkin. "Good meal."

"Are you going to eat those chips?" Drew eyed Roman's plate with hungry eyes.

Roman chuckled and pushed his plate towards the boy. "Knock yourself out, kid."

"Cheers." Drew offered the chips to his brother who scooped off a large handful.

With a happy sigh, Eddie sprinkled a sea of salt over his pile followed by a large squirt of tomato sauce before offering the sauce bottle to Drew.

"What do you have planned for tomorrow?" Abby placed her knife and fork neatly on her plate.

"I've been invited by Dodge to attend the SES meeting tomorrow night." Roman took another swig of his beer.

"Really? I'll be there. I'm a member." Abby poked a strand of hair behind her ear, and bit down on her lower lip for a second before, asking, "Why would Dodge invite you?"

"Apparently I've got skills the SES could use."

"You're only staying a few days." The words were sharp enough to cut through ice.

Trying not to wince, he leaned back in his chair. "I can make myself useful while I'm here."

"I guess." His erstwhile wife looked at the boys who were listening with interest. "These two terrors may as well come along."

"That's what I thought. Give them an understanding on what it takes to build a town and protect a community."

Drew pulled a face. "I've got to study."

Abby smiled and crooked her little finger at him. "Nice try. But it won't work."

"Damn."

"Language," Roman said while Drew rolled his eyes. After a cautious glance at Abby's expression which looked almost as mutinous as Drew's, he thought may as well be hung for a sheep as for a lamb. "In the morning, I'm off to the hardware shop to buy materials for a chicken coop."

Abby's frown turned ferocious and he had to resist the urge to lean over and kiss the wrinkles from her forehead. "You don't have to do that, Roman. I wasn't fishing for help when I mentioned Mrs Miller has chooks she's giving away."

He shrugged. "I know, but I like the idea. Plus, the boys can help me at the weekend."

"I thought we were going kayaking!" cried Eddie in a loud wail, looking up from his chips. Tomato sauce coated his finger-tips.

"That's Sunday," Roman said calmly. "Saturday, Abby has suggested you could join in the local soccer team. And in the afternoon, we need to do something about the gaps around the windows of Abby's house."

"It's a rental," objected Abby, beginning to twirl her wedding ring round and round her finger.

What was she thinking? That he was over-reaching himself? Forcing his way into her life?

A burst of laughter had him turning his head. At a nearby table sat a family of five. Parents, a kid in a high-chair, and another two kids of primary-school age, all sharing a simple evening meal at the local pub.

Like us.

The thought entered Roman's head that this was how life should be, and his heart damn well near cracked apart.

CHAPTER 13

The moon hung low in the sky, a sliver of silver, stark against the inky black. In the quiet of the night, the gentle flow of the river and the lone warble of a magpie ebbed across the fields carried on the mere whisper of a breeze.

Roman drove towards the Bindarra Creek SES building, located at the tail end of River Road and just past the caravan park that sprawled in a haphazard fashion down one side of the Akuna River from Gillies Bridge. With the window of his rental car rolled down, he breathed deeply, enjoying the scents of the night.

A few minutes before seven, he pulled up in the gravel car park that separated the large SES shed from the vicarage which was on the corner of Church Street and River Road. Abby's dusty old Land Rover was parked several vehicles over.

He shook his head, recalling the firm don't-argue-with-me tone she'd used when he'd suggested he pick them up and bring them into town.

She was keeping him at a distance.

And given his was a temporary visit, that was probably the wisest move. Didn't mean he had to like it. He slammed the door shut with unnecessary force. With a zip-up trackie jacket over one arm in case the night turned cold, he strode to the front entrance. The motion detector lights flickered, then lit up the car park. From the door flowed the buzz of many voices, and Roman wiped his boots on the rubber mat before entering.

Glancing around the large rectangular room, Roman recognised quite a few faces. The local SES station was well manned. He nodded as his gaze met that of Harold Westbury who owned the local IGA store. His wife, Nancy who towered over the shorter Harold, waved then bent her head as she listened to old Roy Towns who had a folder clutched under one arm and a fistful of pens in his right hand.

Dan came over and introduced his wife, Alice, as the local park ranger and the owner of a beautiful smile that made her eyes shine.

"Glad you could make it." Dan stretched out his hand.

They shook and Roman smiled.

Dan shouted a greeting as Dodge Myers entered the building at a rush with an elderly Japanese guy by his side. "What took you so long, mate?"

"Kids." Dodge gave a mock grimace. "Kaylee and Tessa had a *'discussion',* shall we call it, about the school dance. Somehow I had to be the referee and ended up being the bad guy!"

Dan laughed.

Dodge looked at Roman and smiled. "Good to see you

here. Meet Maki Fukuka, a close friend of my family. Maki, this is Roman Taylor, the bloke I was telling you about."

Maki and Roman greeted each other.

Roman indicated the people in the hall. "Looks like you have quite the team."

"Yeah." Dodge shoved his hands into his pockets and rocked back on his heels. Sounding proud, he said, "My wife heads the Bindarra Creek Progress Association. She used a portion of the government grant we received to organise a massive fund-raising venture. Check out the result." He grinned. "A brand-new building and up-to-date equipment. We had quite a surge of interest in joining after that, and for newcomers, it's one of the best ways to be integrated into a community. Join a club."

Roman stroked his chin. "With so many members, why do you need more?"

"Always room for one more, mate." Dodge turned around, saying over his shoulder, "Come on. As soon as we've got the chairs out, we'll start our meeting."

"Slave driver," mock-moaned Dan.

Roman followed them over to the side of the hall where plastic chairs were stacked seven high.

"Hey, Roman!"

"Hi, Drew, Eddie." Roman smiled at the boys coming towards him, Eddie in a rush, Drew slouching along. Behind them strolled Abby, dressed in a long-sleeved pink tee shirt and a pair of faded blue jeans tight enough to cause his mouth to go dry.

She smiled, looking happy to see him.

If only that was true.

Other members joined them as they placed the chairs in orderly rows, and it wasn't long before there was the usual shifting about and good-humoured jokes as everyone took their seats.

Roman took a chair on one side of Abby, the boys on her other side. He noted with considerable amusement how Drew attempted to act like he was bored with a lot of eye-rolling and hard-done-by sighs, but the boy shut up and listened intently when Dodge opened the meeting.

A general swell of voices erupted when the members heard how their current commander had resigned without notice. The deputy, a bloke who looked like he was nearing his hundredth year in the land of the living, advised he had no intention of applying for the position. Dodge kept throwing pointed glances in Roman's direction as everyone talked about what they needed in a leader and who they thought might make a good commander of their station.

Abby elbowed him and chuckled softly. "Dodge sure has you in his sights."

"I know." Roman leaned closer, sucking in a lungful of the fragrant jasmine perfume she was so fond of, and whispered, "What could it hurt to give them a hand for a few days?"

She turned so suddenly her face was a breath from his. "Are you serious?"

"I guess I am," he said slowly. "I could fill in until they found the right person."

Her eyebrows rose. "Be careful or you might find it's a permanent position. Dodge is very much Edwina Lette's grandson."

"Would that be so bad?"

Blinking, Abby jerked her gaze to the front. "We've talked about this, Roman. You know my answer."

Anger, hurt, and disappointment boiled to the surface. Roman straightened and before his brain caught up with his body, his hand was in the air.

"Excellent!" Dodge pointed at Roman. "Quieten down, everyone. Lucky for us, we've got a bloke in town who's got considerable experience with rescues and disasters. Stand up, Roman Taylor, and let everyone get a good look at you."

Abby hissed in an annoyed breath.

Roman stood, his chin jutting out. Aware that Drew and Eddie were gaping at him, he turned around and smiled, calling out, "I'm happy to fill in for the short-term."

Dodge began to clap, and others joined in while Abby looked like she wanted to slice him into minced meat.

"Let's move on then. We've got a few items to discuss before we wind up. And since we're all here, let's get in an hour or two of training." Dodge motioned for Roman to join him.

Roman walked to the front, then stood off to the side.

"Dad, you're up next," said Dodge.

Warren Myers pulled down the map of the district that was screwed to the wall and the room fell silent.

Using a laser pointer, Warren stepped away to allow everyone a good look. He indicated an area to the north east of Bindarra Creek and spoke about the recent heavy deluge hitting certain regions. "The north-western slopes of the New England ranges had a good amount of rain recently. Akuna National Park has received a large volume of rainfall over the past three days and the Akuna River is beginning to flow quite strongly."

He looked at Roman. "For your info, mate, the Akuna River is also fed by Bindarra Creek which comes down from the north of the state."

Drawing circles around the small town of Barraba, Warren continued, "Rain has also been falling steadily in this area. I recommend we keep a close eye on these two weather systems. I also suggest we put a message out in the local rag and on our website to warn anyone who is thinking of taking a dip to be cautious."

Roman frowned. "Do you think a flood could be a possibility?"

Warren rubbed his nose. "Hard to say. I realise we're in the grip of another drought at the moment." He addressed the crowd. "But to be on the safe side, and considering Barraba and the national park are being flogged with rain, we should keep an eye on the river levels."

"What about the warm temperatures we've had yesterday and today?" Roman asked.

Warren nodded. "That's what's concerning me the most. According to the Bureau of Meteorology, there is a cold front moving across the state from the interior." He high-lighted Bindarra Creek with his laser pointer. "The storm-chasers group I'm a member of believe we could be in for a hell of a storm. As always, we'll provide updates on a daily basis via our website. Over to you, Dodge."

"Alright. We're going to go over emergency-response training tonight. Team up into groups of five and Roy will pass out the details." Dodge gestured to Roman. "Let's head into the office and go through a few formalities."

As the members formed into groups, Roman took another thoughtful glance at the map. A quiver ran down his spine and he brushed a hand over the pebbling skin at the base of his neck.

Something bad was on its way.

CHAPTER 14

Saturday dawned another delightfully warm day, much to Eddie's mounting excitement. All he could talk of, were the chickens that would soon be running around the yard, and how he was going kayaking. All Drew could do, was tease and torment him, but with a wide grin on his face.

And all Abby could do was smile as the house hummed with energy.

Even a morning spent kicking a soccer ball around a field hadn't dimmed their enthusiasm.

She fed another load of dirty clothes into the washer. From inside, came the low *vroom* of the vacuum cleaner as Drew ran the machine over the carpet while Eddie rattled and clashed dishes in the sink. She marvelled at how easily they'd all fallen into a domestic routine.

Whatever the boys' lives had been like in the foster homes they'd been in, it was obvious they were used to helping out around the house. It must have been very traumatic for the boys to watch their mother's illness progress. They must miss her, terribly. No wonder they were suspicious and had walls the size of China's around their hearts.

But there were moments when she sensed Eddie's desperation to love, to feel loved, to feel safe. Drew was a harder nut to crack, older than his years but beneath, Abby knew he was as vulnerable as his younger brother. They were good kids and deserved better than what life had flung at them so far.

Thinking about the unread email from the association dealing with the boys' foster situation sitting in her inbox, Abby shut the washer door and set the program. She walked out onto the verandah, and spent a moment watching Roman unload building materials from the back of a box trailer he'd rented. It seemed he was hell-bent on building this chicken coop.

She eyed the growing stockpile and remembered the amount of planning and renovating he'd done to their small townhouse all those years ago when they'd believed the world lay at their feet and nothing would go wrong with their dreams. "I hope it's not the Taj Mahal you're building. I'm only getting a couple of chickens."

He looked up, a wide grin on his face and her heart did a somersault.

Why couldn't she stop loving him? It wasn't as if she hadn't tried but one glance from him was all it took for the world to fall away leaving just her and Roman.

The only man she'd ever wanted.

The only man for her.

Folding her arms over her chest, she cleared her throat and walked down the steps. She heard the sounds of the vacuum being turned off, the rumble of the boys' voices and the stomping of feet running through the house. The next second, Eddie and Drew came flying out the door sending it banging against the wall. Pinky barked and raced beside them, as they dashed down the steps and over to the mound of building materials.

"What's all this for?" Drew began to pull aside a roll of wire.

"Good question," Abby murmured.

Roman clucked his tongue at her. "Oh, ye of little faith." He went back to his car and retrieved a satchel from the back seat. Walking towards them, he pulled out an A4 sketch pad with a flourish. "There are the plans I've made for the chicken coop."

"Seriously? You drew up a building plan?" Shaking her head, Abby laughed.

Their eyes met.

The years rolled back and suddenly she was standing with Roman in their old townhouse while he showed her sketches of the plans for the extension, the one that would house their baby.

"Abby."

His voice, low, tender, compassionate pulled her out of the past and into the present.

She blinked.

Drew had shoved his hands into his jeans. Eddie was hugging his waist. Neither boy smiled as they glanced from one adult to the other. They'd stiffened as if ready to run.

Abby met Roman's concerned gaze. The pain in his eyes mirrored the pain in her heart.

"I can forget it." He made as if to shove the pad back into his satchel.

"No, don't. I want to look." Abby drew in a long, steadying breath and the memory faded. She smiled. "I want this chicken coop."

The grins that broke out on the boys' faces were more than a reward, they were a balm, and filled her with a warmth and hope she'd never thought she'd feel again.

"That-a-girl," murmured Roman, pride ringing firm in his voice.

Gesturing for the boys to move closer, he opened his sketch book.

Abby joined them as he pointed out the insulated asphalt roof for all weather protection, the indoor and outdoor areas, the nesting section with a liftable roof and the non-slip ramp leading up to the coop and how long the enclosed run was going to be.

"That is so the Taj Mahal." Gently, Abby tapped the sketch with her forefinger. "It's perfect, Roman."

"I knew you'd love it." He grinned.

Drew gazed around the paddock. "What about foxes?"

"That's a good point," Roman said, his voice warm with approval.

A flush spreading over his face, Drew seemed to stand taller.

Roman toed the roll of wire lying on the ground. "We'll use this high-grade steel mesh around the run and coop, instead of chicken mesh, which foxes can tear open with their jaws."

Drew thought for a moment as he looked at the plans, then said, "What about over the top? Cats could climb the wire."

"That's an excellent point, Drew." Roman smiled. "I could do with a hand building this thing."

"I guess I could help." Drew's tone might have been grudging but Abby wasn't fooled. Judging by the way he kept eyeing off the materials, he was as mad keen to start as Roman.

"What about me? Can't I help?" Eddie asked, his brown eyes as round as saucers.

"You both can." Roman handed his sketch pad and satchel to Abby. "But first, we need to caulk up the cracks letting in the draughts in that house or you'll all turn to icie pops."

Abby clutched the satchel to her chest. "And I need to get the meat out to defrost for dinner tonight. But I'd love to help with the coop, if you need another pair of hands, Roman."

"Always, babe. Always."

Always.

Once upon a time, she'd believed in an 'always' for them. But that was years ago, and this was now.

The sound of Roman's laughter reached her. She paused on the top step, her hand clenching on the railing.

Always.

If only his words could be true.

CHAPTER 15

Abby's Land Rover was packed to the hilt, eskies filled with food, water bottles, a jerry-can of spare diesel, towels, swimming gear, and towing the rented box trailer where the two double-seated kayaks and paddles were strapped down.

"Can't believe this weather we're having," Abby said as she neared the car park at the lower western end of the Akuna National Park.

"It's magic," Roman agreed from where he sat in the passenger seat. Another wonderful aspect of his personality that she loved so much, he had no qualms about women driving, being equals in life, or taking charge. "How fast do you think the river is flowing?"

Abby shot him a quick glance as the car bounced over a pothole. "Not sure. Hopefully, since we're at the lower edges of the park and not up at the top of the gorge, she won't be moving too swiftly. But there are plenty of deep, calm pools amongst the rocks where we can take a swim if the river is too dangerous for a paddle."

"Oh, man! I thought we were going kayaking," whined Eddie.

"Cut it out, bro. You heard what they said at the meeting the other night about the rain and stuff."

"But …"

"One thing at a time." Roman interrupted the boys with his firm voice. "Let's not count our chickens before they hatch."

Both boys sniggered and did a bit of play-pushing and shoving in the back seat.

"We're coming up to the campsite," Abby said calmly, and notched down a gear as she swung the car into the parking area several metres from the campgrounds.

"Looks choice." Drew craned his neck this way and that looking out every window.

"There're only a couple of campers here," Roman said, indicating the two tents, "which means we won't have to arm wrestle anyone to use the BBQ. Boys, give us a hand please getting our gear out of the car."

"We're all over it. Come on, Eddie," cried Drew as he yanked open his door and jumped to the ground.

His brother tumbled out after him.

Abby's gaze met Roman's and they grinned. Only a few days and already one of the boys was mimicking Roman's words. They both climbed from the car, Abby pocketing the keys.

They decided to situate their picnic spot on the grassy flats beside the river, and in the shade of a bottle-brush tree. Abby spread the picnic blanket while Roman and the boys set down the esky and water, then they all carried the kayaks and paddles to the river's sandy edge.

"What'll we do first?" Eddie hopped about from foot to foot.

"Sunscreen and maybe a visit to the toilet block. I thought we'd go for a bush walk to the look-out, then a paddle."

Roman smiled. "I like your plan, hon."

"That's settled then." Kneeling on the rug, Abby opened her large, canvas beach bag and brought out the sunscreen lotion which she handed over to Eddie first, watching as he slathered his face, before asking him to pass it onto his brother.

Drew rubbed the lotion onto the back of his neck then gave the bottle to Roman.

"Thanks, mate." Roman slapped on the sunscreen and handed it back to Abby.

Abby smoothed the cream over her face and rose to her feet. "Meet you back here in ten."

"I've already got my swimming trunks on under my board shorts." Roman dug into his backpack and brought out his Ricoh camera. "While you lot get yourselves sorted, I'll take a few shots of the camping area and the river."

Smiling, Abby picked up her beach bag. "Still enjoy photography?"

"Yeah, but not as much as painting." He shrugged. "I like to paint from the photos that I take rather than doing in-situ sketches."

"Do you have any of your paintings with you?"

"No. I only brought an overnight bag. Thought I'd buy some boards and paints from the newsagency, and start working on a piece this week."

"I can't wait to see it."

Roman laughed. "Don't get your hopes up. I'm strictly an amateur."

"Maybe, but I bet you'll be awesome." Sending him a wink, Abby strolled off, aware of Roman's gaze following her. A delicious thrill warmed her as she recalled the flash of heat in his eyes.

It seemed that five years had done little to dim the attraction they felt for each other. The only question was, did she intend to act on it? The wisest course of action would be to ignore the pull, and not get physically involved.

But the problem is – I'm lonely. I missed him.

She missed his smiles, the tenderness he used to show every morning when he'd wake her with a gentle kiss, his solid presence in their home, the knack he had of knowing something needed to be fixed before it became an issue, and the amazing meals he'd cook, the wonderful togetherness they'd forged before their world had fallen apart.

Not all my memories are bad. When did I start to forget the good times?

Thoughtful, Abby waved a hello to the other campers as she passed. A young couple were sprawled on blankets on the ground, faces turned to the sun. A family of four were seated on one of the timber tables and benches, enjoying morning tea and cake. With lots of shade from tall trees and a flat area on which to pitch tents, this would be the perfect place to camp for a few days whilst enjoying the river and national park.

A few minutes later, and she headed back to their picnic site.

Her spirits lifted as she spotted Drew and Eddie

standing quietly beside Roman as he took a picture of a small flock of lorikeets feeding on the nectar of the blossoms in a wattle tree. They rose in a flutter of wings, squawking like flustered chickens when she approached.

Roman stowed his camera into his backpack and slipped the bag over his shoulders. "Ready?"

Abby nodded. "Let's go." She traded her beach bag for a smaller and lighter backpack into which she'd placed several water bottles and a first-aid kit. She plopped her wide-brimmed cloth hat over her hair, and brandished a map. "The walk to the lookout should take us about thirty or forty minutes."

Eddie's lower lip drooped. "I want to go for a paddle."

"And we will, hon. Later. You'll love it when we reach the top. I'll pop your towels into my bag in case we want a swim somewhere on the way." She bent down to grab the boys' towels.

"No, I'll take them, Abby." Drew shoved the towels into his school backpack and threw a cap at his brother. "Put this on, Eddie."

His brother rolled his eyes but slapped his hat on his head.

Touched at this show of thoughtfulness, Abby smiled at him. "Thanks, Drew."

He ducked his head and kicked at the ground with his runner.

"Ready, boys?" Roman asked and when they nodded, he grinned. "Let's go, then."

They set off, Abby in the lead. The boys walked behind, pointing when they spotted a bird and then a rock wallaby that watched them from a safe distance.

Roman joined Abby's side and linked a hand through hers. "Have you been here before?"

"Once, last year when we had the first scavenger challenge. The last of the clues was up near the guest house. I wish I'd come back before now. There's so much to explore and do here."

He took the park map from her and scanned it. "Wow. I never realised." With a wry grin on his face, he admitted, "I usually check out places before I go but for some reason, I didn't google this park."

"It's not very well known. But that makes it all the more special to the locals." She looked around and addressed the boys. "The river runs fourteen kilometres almost through the middle of the park. When we get to the top of the gorge, you'll see massive granite boulders and the rapids where the river falls back down into the valley."

"Did you hear that, Drew?" Eddie breathed in awe. "We can go white-water rafting!"

Roman cleared his throat. "No way. Not until you've got a lot more experience with kayaking. Let's take it one step at a time."

"Forget it, Eddie. We won't be here that long." Drew met Abby's stare in a challenging manner. But behind his mild aggression was a question he couldn't ask. He broke his gaze and stuffed his hands in his pockets.

Unable to make a promise she wasn't certain she could keep, Abby turned her blurry eyes to the track ahead, hating the heavy silence that had fallen. Drew and Eddie were proving to be very special and very likeable kids, ones who deserved a happy home.

Her thoughts returned to that damn unopened email.

She'd recognised the logo and known immediately it was in response to her temporary fostering application of the boys. The last time she'd made an application to do with a child, the result had been devastating for her and her marriage.

Even thinking about the email now made her hands clammy and her heart race. She hadn't mentioned its existence to Roman knowing he'd want to open the damn thing.

What if the organisation wanted the boys back sooner than expected?

How would she feel?

But maybe it would be better if she did send them back now. Before they all became far too comfortable in a life that would end in a few weeks anyway.

Her breathing became choppy, her mind fogged.

"Hey." Roman tugged her hand. "Anything the matter?"

"No. All good." She shook her head and forced a smile. "Race you to the top."

She set off at a run. There was a momentary hesitation then she heard Drew's *'whoop!'* as Roman and the boys thundered after her.

Forget about later. Enjoy the day.

She raced them to the lookout.

The track wound through the bush and every so often she saw a glimpse of the cliff walls opposite and a glint of water. Drew passed her and then Roman, leaving her and Eddie to chug along the rear. Eventually the trail widened out into a clearing where there were a set of bush dunnies and a small camping area.

"I win!" yelled Drew, jumping up and down, fist in the air.

Roman clapped him on the back then flung his head back, breathing deeply.

Abby puffed to a halt and leaned over to relieve the stitch in her side while Eddie pulled out a bottle and chugged down some water.

"That was fun." Drew grinned. "Now where?"

Still breathless, Abby pointed to where the trail started again.

Roman touched her shoulder. His face glistened with sweat. "We're getting old, babe."

Abby laughed. "That we are." She nodded to where the boys were heading. "I think you should go first. The track leads quite close to the cliff edge a bit farther on."

"I'm all over it. Hey, guys! Wait up!" He rushed after the kids.

Pressing a hand to her aching side, Abby followed.

A few minutes later the trail led up to where a timber look-out had been built into the side of the cliff. Abby joined the boys and Roman, and they all admired the pink and purple granite boulders that formed the gorge and then spent several minutes gazing at the river rushing beneath.

Turning, she pointed out the cottage built from local rock that clung to the buff as if it had grown out of the rocks. Orange gums and white box woodland trees formed a shady backdrop.

"Who lives there?" asked Eddie. "Can we go inside?"

"No, we can't, it's a holiday house. Someone could be staying here."

Roman raised his eyebrows. "Perfect place to spend a few days while exploring the park." He winked at Abby. "Or a great honeymoon spot."

Heat flooded her face. Her lips twitched as she fought back her smile. "If we walk farther along, the track comes out at some rock pools. Does anyone want to go for a swim?"

Eddie folded his arms. "I want to go kayaking."

"You, Eddie …" Roman ruffled the boy's head, causing his hat to fall over his eyes. "Are like a broken record."

Eddie grinned and pushed back his cap. "What's a record?"

"You're so dumb." Drew poked his brother in the back.

"Let's have a quick dip then head down to our camp," Abby suggested.

"Only if it means we can go for a kayak," Eddie pleaded.

Abby laughed, meeting Roman's twinkling eyes. "Definitely a broken record. But, yes, we will spend the remainder of the day on the river, kayaking."

"Yay!" Eddie shouted and did a victory dance around his brother.

After cooling off in a swimming hole, they returned to the picnic area where they had a light lunch of cold meat sandwiches and slices of hummingbird cake. Roman pulled out his sketch book and began to draw.

"Are you working on a painting, Roman? Can I see?" teased Abby as she packed away the remains of lunch.

Silver eyes glinting, he glanced up. "Nope. And nope. Not yet anyway. It's a surprise."

"A surprise. Cool." Drew leaned over to take a peek.

But grinning, Roman shook his head and closed the book. "Later, dude. When I've finished."

It wasn't long before they were laughing as they paddled down the river in the kayaks.

All-in-all, it was a perfect day, Abby decided while they packed up their gear as the sun sank below the trees. They drove home, the boys falling asleep in the rear of the car, Roman scrolling through the photos he'd taken, and Abby, Abby daring to dream of more wonderful days to come.

All thoughts of the unread email had fled from her mind.

CHAPTER 16

"Don't forget to pack your jackets today. There's a storm forecast for this afternoon," Abby warned as she handed over lunch bags on Thursday morning.

"So what?" Drew shrugged. "It's just a bit of rain."

"Nevertheless, go back and get your coat." Abby pointed down the hall.

Grumbling, Drew slouched off.

"I've already got mine." Eddie beamed.

"Douche bag!" yelled Drew from the bedroom.

"Okay. Okay. No fighting." Smiling, Abby picked up her keys and police jacket then as an afterthought went to the pantry and shook out extra kibble into Pinky's dry dog food bowl. "Everyone in the car. I'll only be a few moments."

She rushed out the back door, and across the yard to the chicken coop Roman and the boys had finished on Tuesday afternoon. After checking the coop's latch was secured, Abby hurried to the barn where she wedged open the barn door. If a storm did eventuate, she wanted to ensure the door wouldn't blow shut. That way, Geronimo could move freely in and out of the barn as he chose. She took a few extra minutes to pluck an apple from a sack hanging from a nail on the wall and went over to where her horse was grazing. He raised his head at her approach and nickered softly.

"Good boy. Sorry I haven't spent much time with you lately. This weekend. I promise." Smiling, she fed him the apple then ran her hand over his neck and fondled his ears. One last pat and she returned to the house.

After locking up, she trotted down the steps to the police paddy wagon. Once inside, she told the boys to strap in then started the engine.

"Like this doesn't suck, turning up to school in the back of a cop car," Drew grumbled. "Why can't we use your car?"

"Because I was on-call last night. Could be worse." Abby flashed him a grin over her shoulder as she headed for the road. "I could work for a funeral director. You could turn up in a hearse."

Drew laughed.

"Like *The Addams Family*!" shouted Eddie, bouncing in his seat.

"You're such a douche." Drew shoved him.

Before an argument could escalate, Abby intervened, "Tell me, how's school going? Drew, you first." After checking for on-coming cars, she swung onto the road and accelerated.

"It's okay," he said in a grudging tone.

"I thought you could invite a school mate over this weekend."

He was quiet for a moment before he answered. "I'd like that. Can I invite more than one?"

"Sure." Abby smiled.

"What about me? I want to invite someone," said Eddie.

"Why not? The more the merrier." Abby tapped a finger on the steering wheel. "I know. We'll have a barbeque. Let's see. Saturday you've both got soccer. How about Sunday?"

"Sounds cool. I'll ask Ethan and Noah," Drew said.

"They're on your soccer team too, aren't they?"

"Yeah. Ethan's parents have this hobby farm out of town somewhere and Noah lives with his mum in Wattle Drive."

"Let them know I can pick them up and run them home if needed."

"Thanks." Drew leaned forward to rest his arms on the seat in front. "You could invite their parents, too. Be a good way for you and Roman to meet people. You don't seem to get out much."

Out of the mouths of babes.

Abby turned Drew's words over in her mind. Up to now, she'd spent her leisure time mainly alone, doing chores, riding Geronimo, or filling her hours with SES training. Rarely had she accepted an invitation to someone's home.

Being that close to those living happy family lives brought back too many memories of what she'd lost and what she could never have.

She chanced a quick look in the rear-vision mirror meeting Drew's concerned gaze. He was right. It was time she really became part of this town.

And the boys needed to know what it meant to be part of a community too.

She lifted her chin, ignoring the quiver of something like anxiety along her spine. "I don't know their parents."

"Not a problem. I'll get my mates to ask for you." Drew tapped a finger on her shoulder, then quickly withdrew his hand. "It'll do you good. And Roman, too."

Tears stung Abby's eyes.

God, this boy is too old for his years. Bless him.

"Thank you," she muttered.

He shrugged like it was no big deal but when her gaze met his in the rear-vision mirror, his expression revealed genuine concern.

"I want to ask Gav. He's got a pony. He goes riding with Kaylee, Gillian, Ray and June. They go to the pony club. Gav said I can come over to his place and ride his horse anytime. Can I, Abby? But what if I fall off? Gav might laugh at me." Eddie's voice trembled.

Abby slowed down a gear as she approached Gillies Bridge. "I'll give you some lessons on Geronimo. He may be big but he's as gentle as a lamb."

"Yay! I'm gonna ride a horse. I'd like to join the pony club. But won't I need my own horse, Abby?"

Eddie's excitement was contagious.

Abby grinned. "I think you can hire a pony from the riding school."

"Or I could get a job. Mow lawns or something. That way I can save up for a pony of my own."

Abby's heart swelled and without thinking, said, "Sounds a sensible plan."

Drew growled, "Can it, Eddie. We're not staying here. Remember?"

Of course, they weren't staying. How could she get so carried away?

Chastened, Abby chanced a glance over her shoulder. Drew had turned his head away, staring out the window, and Eddie was slumped in his seat. There were definitely tears glistening in his eyes. He rubbed a hand under his nose while Drew scowled at the passing scenery.

Drew was right, their stay here wasn't forever. It was cruel of her to act otherwise.

Abby thought of the unopened email still sitting in her inbox.

And felt as low as dirt.

CHAPTER 17

Another day at the office, Abby thought as the hours rushed by. Already she'd attended to a neighbour's dispute over their dividing fence then dropped by the vicarage for a chat with Florrie Miller. As the clouds grew steadily darker overhead, she'd driven through every street in town, twice, checking for a dark blue Lexus convertible.

With no luck.

Now mid-afternoon, Abby ducked instinctively as another crash of thunder rolled over the cloud-laden skies as the storm gathered strength. "Wow. That sounds close."

AJ rushed to the police station's front door and peered outside. "Get a load of this, Abby! Awesome. The lightning is striking just seconds apart." He snapped a shot with his phone before jumping back as an almighty crack resounded through the building. "Woah!"

The floor shuddered and Abby grabbed the edge of her desk, her breath hitching. She checked her watch. Not even three in the afternoon, and yet it was so dark outside the street lights had flicked on.

The boys should still be in school. Were they safe there, or should she ask Roman to pick them up and take them home? She bit her lip and reached for her mobile, scrolling through her favourite apps until she found the weather site.

"That definitely hit something." Riley surged to his feet, motioning for Abby to do the same. "Let's check it out. AJ, you man the phones."

But Abby hung back, shaking her head. "Maybe we should wait until the storm passes. The weather system is quite intense."

She showed Riley her phone screen where the radar image depicted a dark red mass sitting directly over the town.

"Bloody hell. We're about to be hammered."

No sooner had Riley spoken than the heavens opened up.

Abby clapped her hands over her ears and shouted over the onslaught on the building's tin roof, "Is that rain?"

"Nah!" yelled AJ from where he was near the front door, his Caribbean accent coming through in his excitement. "It's hail. OMG! Dis is some serious storm."

"I knew that warm weather we've had these past few days was been too good to be true," shouted Riley.

AJ made a dash out the door to return a couple of seconds later holding his cupped hands in front of him. "Look at the size of tis ting."

Abby crossed the room to examine the two hail stones

AJ held. "Holy smokes! That's got to be at least six centimetres wide!"

"If that hits someone on the head, that could cause serious injury." Riley planted his hands on his belt. "AJ, shut that bloody door."

Flinching as another earth-shattering crack resounded from outside, Abby scuttled over to her desk and brought up the Bureau of Meteorology site. Heart in her mouth, she read the warnings for the district within a fifteen-kilometre radius: winds gusts predicted up to one hundred and twenty kilometres per hour, dry lightning, and heavy hail. Very little rain though.

AJ shut the front door and immediately the din lessened to a bearable level. He ran a hand over his cropped, black curls.

Riley leaned over Abby's shoulder and read her screen. His finger traced the radar image. "I reckon we've got about two hours minimum before this low-pressure system moves farther north and away from town."

He looked at Abby. "You're right, though. Isn't much we can do until its passed. We'll have to ride it out and hope people have got the sense to stay put. AJ, I want you to monitor the phones. Abby, you're on the radio comms, and listen for any squawks from the ambos or firies. I'll keep an eye on our station's Facebook page as well as Bindarra's Facebook page in case someone posts they need help there."

"Yes, boss," said Abby.

"Rightio, Sarge," sang out AJ.

Senior Sergeant Morgan took his seat as he tapped out a message on his mobile. A quick glance at AJ showed he was also doing the same.

Abby settled down in front of the radio network comms terminal and fished out her mobile. She texted Roman to pick up the boys as soon as the hail stopped. A second later, a message pinged back *'Stay safe.'* Only two words, but sufficient to give her a case of the warm and fuzzies. Smiling, she brought up the weather app again.

It wasn't long before the calls began to flow through to the station.

"This is bloody ridiculous. Us sitting here useless as tits on a bull." Riley drummed his fingers on the desk.

Abby chewed the end of her pen. "If only this hail would stop." Then a thought struck her. "Riot gear. What idiots we are. Sarge, if we use the riot helmets you brought back from Sydney ..."

"Of course!" Riley surged to his feet and raced to the backroom where extra gear was stored.

Abby followed hot on his heels, entering the room as the senior sergeant unlocked the steel-meshed gate and strode to the bank of lockers. Removing three aging but still serviceable riot helmets, he tossed one over to Abby and grinned.

"Let's move."

"Yes, sir!" Strapping on the helmet, Abby rushed back to the front office. "Sorry, AJ, but we'll need you here. I'll take the paddy wagon while Sarge drives the highway patrol car."

Swinging into his chair, Riley pulled up the calls they'd received, then divided them into levels of urgency and sections of the town. He printed out two lists, handing one for the southern part of town to Abby.

The lights fizzed then went out, along with their computer screens.

"Damn. Power's down." Face grim, Riley looked over at Abby. "My first stop will be the IGA store. The roof's collapsed and not everyone's been accounted for. Listen, Abby, I want updates every fifteen minutes, and AJ? You keep logging those calls, and funnel them through to us via our phones. Let's keep the radios open for emergencies only."

Nodding, Abby grabbed her keys and shrugged into a bulletproof vest to protect her shoulders and chest from injury. Striding to the door, she called out a 'cheerio' to AJ as she double checked her duty belt then slapped her inside breast pocket, ensuring her mobile was tucked in nice and tight. She muttered a brief thanks to the powers that be that gel belts had been issued to alleviate backpain problems that were accentuated following long work shifts. She had a feeling today was going to be one of those days.

The instant she left the shelter of the station, hail struck hard and heavy on her helmet and shoulders. Her ears rang from the pinging of impact, and the sections of her shoulders not covered by the vest throbbed as hail stones plummeted from the sky like rounded daggers. The wind was a roar of anger pummelling her as she staggered to the paddy wagon, and she had to wrestle against its force to drag the driver's door open.

Panting, she finally subsided behind the wheel. The door slammed shut but inside the cabin the storm seemed louder.

Turning on the engine, the headlights, and windscreen wipers, she edged out onto Court Street, heading for the first name at the top of her list.

An elderly couple out on Wilgara Avenue were

trapped inside their house after a tree had fallen through the lounge room roof. Abby leaned forward and squinted through the windscreen as she drove as fast as she dared down the road, blue and white lights flashing.

Hail smashed against the glass. Tiny cracks appeared and feathered from one side of the windscreen to the other.

"Perfect. Just perfect," Abby growled through her teeth, turning the wheel to the left, then to the right to avoid loose debris blowing hither and yonder on the wind.

A sheet of corrugated iron sailed through the air. Leaves and twigs twirled like demented dancers, limiting visibility. Larger branches scudded across the road, making driving dangerous.

She cringed as a lawn chair somersaulted out from her left-hand side. It skidded across the bonnet, flipped into the air then disappeared from sight.

Five heart-pounding minutes later, she pulled up in front of a battered house where a couple of Harley Davidsons were parked well away from any trees. Two burly blokes, one tall and the other short, and both with motorbike helmets on their heads, were clambering over a massive tree trunk embedded in the building's crushed-in iron roof.

Leaving the headlights on, Abby struggled out of the car then moved to the rear doors. From beneath one of the bench side seats, she dragged a large metal box and opened the lid.

Chainsaw in hand, she strode towards the house, calling out, "Hey guys! I come bearing a gift!"

"You bloody beauty," bellowed the tall bloke when he turned around and spotted her.

Abby stiffened for a moment as she recognised him and then let the tension go. Shawn Hills, male nurse currently working at Bindarra Creek Hospital and who had priors. He'd spent eight years in a minor security prison for a robbery gone wrong when the house he and his best pal had been attempting to burgle had gone up in flames courtesy of a gas stove inadvertently left on by the owner. Instead of scarpering off, they'd risked their lives and successfully rescued the old lady and her cat.

The incident had turned their lives around. They'd done their time, and finished their high school education while inside and upon their release, worked part-time jobs while they obtained their degrees at Newcastle University. They'd moved to town two years ago where they'd soon fitted right into this close-knit community.

Still, Abby made it her mission to drop into their small cottage every so often for a chinwag, and to make sure they weren't tempted to stray off the short and narrow.

Wiping blood from a gash on his cheek, Shawn smacked his companion on the back and hollered, "Leslie, mate, we've got company. Want me to handle that thing, love?"

"Yeah. Good idea. Leslie and I'll haul the cut timber out of the way." Abby handed the chainsaw over. "Heard anything from inside?"

He nodded. "The old fellow sounds a bit weak. Reckons his leg is broken. His old girl reckons she's all good, though dunno if that's true. She could be trying to stay positive for her hubby."

"Let's start then. Take it slow. We don't want you cutting through any electricity wires."

"Hell no!"

Fifteen minutes later, hail still stormed from the sky and Abby a lather of sweat beneath her heavy clothing and helmet. Her frustration mounted. "We need a bigger chainsaw. This thing isn't making much headway."

"Need some help, babe?" called a familiar and welcome voice.

Abby looked over her shoulder and grinned as Roman bounded towards her, holding a much larger heavy-duty chainsaw in his hands. From the SES twin-cab ute behind him, a bunch of guys piled out. All were decked out in their safety outfits and helmets.

When he came closer, she called, "Where are the boys?"

"Safe at the SES station." Roman's gaze tracked the direction of her torch. "How they doing in there?"

"I think we need to move fast."

"Gotcha."

In a few seconds, he had the team and the two recreational bikies working seamlessly under his direction as he wielded the chainsaw and the others used chains, picks, and shovels to remove the tree and its debris.

It took more than twenty minutes to cut away the trunk sufficiently to make a passage into the house. Abby gave thanks they had a nurse with them, as Shawn had to treat the elderly couple on the scene before they could be moved into the rear of the paddy wagon. The ambulance was tied up on the other side of town. The front awning of the IGA store had crumpled beneath the weight of hailstones, injuring several people.

About to swing into the car, Abby paused as Roman bounded up to her window.

"We still make a good team." His direct gaze pinned her in place, demanding a straight answer.

"Yes, we do." No point in denying the obvious. Smiling, she started the engine. "Where are you off to next?"

Roman checked his mobile before responding. "Dodge and Warren and their team are handling the crisis at the IGA. I've got another two teams dealing with several houses missing tiles from their roofs. Fig Tree Lodge is one of them. After we tarp these old folks' roof, thought I'd take this latest call for help. Vicarage is minus some sheeting iron. And we've got a couple of calls from the caravan park that need attending to."

"The damage bill from this storm is going to be huge." Abby bit her lip.

Roman nodded. "No getting around that, babe. But we're doing our best to minimise it."

"I know you are." She slid in behind the wheel. "I'll catch you later. I may see you at the church. I need to go there next. Stay safe."

Quick as a whip, Roman leaned in and captured her chin in his hand. Then he lowered his head giving her a kiss as tender and light as candy floss.

His lips were exactly as she remembered, warm, soft, and addictive. Abby could feel herself melting, her bones dissolving, and a deep ache for more yearned in her heart.

Recalling the injured waiting in the back of the wagon, she pulled away. "We'll finish this later."

"I'll hold you to that. Stay safe, hon." He stepped back, gave her a wave, and disappeared into the storm.

CHAPTER 18

The hail ceased as abruptly as it had begun. The wind eased to a stiff breeze and overhead, the clouds remained sullen and threatening. Roman looked up from where he was perched on a ladder braced against the vicarage side wall and assessed the night sky.

Was the storm over?

Or was this a lull before another hit the town?

It was the least of his worries, and he didn't have time to check the weather app on his phone. They needed to get this tarp in place then do a quick search to see if they could find the missing sheets of iron and secure them to prevent them from damaging other properties. With luck, they wouldn't be far from the house.

He called out to Jake Morgan, the local vet, who was balanced on the roof, to hoist the tarp up further. After another fifteen minutes of sweating, hauling, and tugging, they had the covering in position. It took another eight minutes to tie it down before Roman could descend the ladder.

Upon reaching the ground, he paused and rotated his shoulder blades. He hadn't been joking when he'd mentioned to Abby the physical demands of his rescue job were finally taking a toll on his body.

He turned around and braced the ladder as Jake climbed down with ease.

Hunter Sullivan came around the corner of the house, another blue tarp balanced on his shoulder. "Finished, mate?"

"Yes. All done here. Where you off too?"

"Thought if it was okay with you, Jake and me would head over to the caravan park."

"No problems. Update the station before you go."

"Will do. What about yourself?"

"I'll pack away this gear then go over to the church. Mrs Miller and the rector went there more than an hour ago and haven't returned home."

"Give us a call if you need us, mate, and we'll head straight back."

"Thanks, Hunter. We've got a de-briefing meeting later tonight. I want all teams there to provide a status update on where we're at with damage control."

"You're the boss." Hunter gave a cheeky wink and, whistling, strode off with the vet.

Roman turned off the emergency floodlight and generator, then packed them in the boot of his rental car before returning for the ladder, ropes, a bag of plastic ties, and the spare tarp. The newly obtained emergency response light storm vehicle was in the hands of the two Myer blokes, dealing with the IGA store crisis.

If he stayed in Bindarra, Roman would be on call twenty-four-seven. He'd be part of a community, and certainly doing his bit to protect a town and its people. It was a great opportunity and a natural fit for him, considering his current job.

If they purchased the house Abby rented, he could work on extending the living areas. Add another bedroom, update the bathroom. He wouldn't mind replacing the kitchen with a brand new one, plus a sunroom could be built off the eastern side. Then he'd build himself and the boys, a decent sized man-cave. His fingers itched to get back to his sketch book.

He'd be able to work on his painting and play an active part in those two boys' lives. But more than that, he'd be with Abby.

A good life. The mere thought gave him a sense of deep fulfilment.

Was it a pipe dream?

In the end, it all came down to his relationship with Abby.

Could they make a go of it again?

And should they pull two vulnerable boys into their lives on the chance that their marriage wouldn't disintegrate, again?

Shaking his head, Roman shelved the uncertainty of his future while he secured the ladder and remaining gear in the trailer. For now, he had a job to do, and that meant he had to track down the reverend and his wife.

Flicking on a torch, he walked through the vicarage garden that had been pulverised by hail, and vaulted over the stone wall that separated the house from the church. With no streetlights, the darkness would have been absolute if not for his torch. Quickly, he side-hopped over a fallen tree branch and continued along the gravel path that led to the front of the church.

An impressive building, he thought as he paused and shone the light over the façade. He squinted, attempting to examine the tower and battlements but his torch wasn't powerful enough to reach that far. But the beam did catch the broken glass of the window about two thirds up the tower face.

That's a shame.

He understood the stained-glass windows were something of a passion for the reverend. Roman swept the light over the front steps, his eyebrows rising when he noted the church doors stood open.

"Hello? Anyone there? Vicar? Mrs Miller, are you here?" he called.

No one responded.

Nevertheless, Roman mounted the three steps and entered the building. Careful to avoid the broken glass scattered over the floor, he walked up and down the aisles, scanning each row as he passed. A pile of hymn books lay scattered over the floor as if knocked from a pew.

Where were the Millers?

He trotted back down the steps and stood a moment listening. But it was hard to pin-point any indication of human activity with the wind whistling around the building. About to walk the church perimeter, he stopped when his mobile rang.

The caller ID revealed Abby, and he couldn't believe how his spirit sang at the sight of her name. "Hey, babe."

"Hi, Roman. Are you still at the vicarage?"

"Yes. I may be a while yet and there's a meeting later at the SES station."

"If you're hungry, I thought we could meet up for a quick meal at the pub. I could order ahead, grab the boys …?" Her voice trailed off suggestively.

Food. The very thought made his taste buds water as he realised just how hungry he was. "Sounds great. I'm going to …"

A gun shot cut through the gusting wind.

Instinctively, he sank into a crouch.

"*Holy smokes!* Roman, are you okay?" Abby yelled over the phone, her voice rising with each word she spoke.

"I'm fine. Yeah. That definitely was a gun, sounded like a rifle and close to the church. I'm going to check it out."

"No! Wait for me! I'll be there in two minutes tops." She rang off.

Not one to waste time, Roman straightened and pocketed his phone. He'd check the rear of the church while he waited for Abby. But if his ears hadn't deceived him, that shot had come from the direction of the cemetery.

Ninety seconds later, car headlights swept up the road. The vehicle stopped suddenly in a savage spurt of gravel.

Roman jogged from the side of the church to meet Abby rushing up the path. He opened his arms and she fell into them.

Her head nestled on his chest and he breathed in her floral scent, enjoying and loving the feel of her body so close to his. It had been so long, too long. And damn, if it didn't feel like coming home.

"Roman." Her voice ended on a hiccup.

Touched, he brushed a tear from her cheek and pressed a quick kiss to her soft lips. "All good, babe. I'm sure the shot came from the cemetery. Haven't heard a peep since."

Nodding, she pulled away, her training coming to the fore as her hand rested on her gun holster. She pulled a torch off her duty belt and flicked it on, saying wryly, "I know we'll present more of a target this way, but that cemetery is a minefield at night. Fallen stones and sunken graves all over the place. I don't care for a broken ankle."

"Same." Brandishing is own torch, Roman made to move off, pushing her behind him.

With a chuckle, she forged ahead, pushing *him* behind *her*. "I've got a vest. You haven't. Stay behind me, Roman."

"Will do."

In silence, they walked out of the church grounds, across Wattle Drive, and into the cemetery. Towering pine trees stood sentry. The wind howled through the trees like a lonely dog.

"What a God-awful noise," Abby muttered in a low voice.

"Yeah, the spooks will be out tonight for sure."

"Don't say that. Gives me the creeps."

But he heard the smile in her voice.

They stopped behind a monstrosity of a monument to listen, but it was hard to hear over the moaning wind.

"Did you hear footsteps over there?" Abby pointed to the north side of the block then turned her head abruptly.

Clothing rustled, only a few metres from where they stood.

Motioning for Roman to remain behind her, Abby swept her torch to the left. Heart racing, he merged his torchlight with hers, widening the field of vision.

Crosses. Headstones. Even a ledger grave marker, its shiny black marble reflecting off the glint of torch-light.

A shadow fluttered between the graves.

Abby drew in a sharp breath as she swung her torch over the area in front of her.

Roman heard the snap of leather as she released her gun from her holster with her other hand.

"Stop! Police! Lower your weapon!" she ordered.

"Abby? Is that you?" quavered a voice Roman recognised.

"Mrs Miller?" Abby said in a softer tone. "Step into the light where we can see you."

"Oh, my goodness!" Hands held high above her head, her eyes popping from their sockets, Florrie Miller inched into view.

"She doesn't appear to be carrying," Abby muttered. Nevertheless, her hand remained on the butt of her pistol as she raised her voice. "Who fired that shot?"

"Well, I'm not exactly certain …"

"Mrs Miller. Is the Reverend out here with you?"

The elderly woman moved closer. "Can I put my hands down now?"

Roman stepped forward and checked the area behind her with his torch. Turning his head, he said to Abby, "I think she's alone."

"My hands …?"

"Yes. Yes." Sounding exasperated, Abby waved her torch at her and shoved her gun back into its holster.

"Thank you, dear. It's surprisingly tiring holding your arms in the air." She peered around and met Roman's gaze. "Well, look here. If it isn't your lovely husband."

Roman smiled. "Mrs Miller, we've finished tarping your roof."

"How wonderful. Thankyou."

"The shot, Mrs Miller. Does the Reverend have your rifle?" Abby prodded.

Florrie frowned. "I doubt it. We came over to inspect the church and he didn't have my gun then. Poor Jonas, the window upset him … All those hours of raising money to restore the glass to its original condition." She folded her hands together in a beseeching manner.

"Never mind the window. Where is your husband? Does he have a gun?"

To their right, footsteps pounded over the earth.

"Thieves! Robbers!" hollered Reverend Miller.

Another shot cracked through the air.

"Bloody hell!" Roman grabbed his wife's arm and yanked her to the ground.

"Jonas! What are you doing?" yelled Mrs Miller as she took off with surprising speed, considering her age.

Abby pulled out of his grasp and sprung to her feet, giving chase.

"This is so crazy. Abby, get back here!" Scowling, Roman raced after her.

Footsteps slapped along a concrete path, then faded.

Abby veered towards the southern edge of the property.

In the distance came the wail of police sirens.

The calvary was on its way.

Together, Abby and Roman sprinted around a hedge and staggered to a halt.

Sitting on a timber bench was the Reverend wearing

his dressing gown and sheepskin Ugg slippers, and holding hands with his wife seated beside him.

"Florrie. Reverend," panted Abby. "Where's the gun?"

"What gun, Senior Constable?" Mrs Miller tilted her head to one side and gave a good impression of a bewildered old woman. "I've got no idea what you're talking about."

"The gun. All of us heard a gun," Abby gritted through her teeth.

Mrs Miller turned to her husband. "Do you see a gun anywhere, Jonas?"

He shook his head and gave a toothy smile.

"Bloody hell," Roman muttered into his wife's ear. "They've stashed it somewhere."

"I know," she whispered back. "We'll have to look for it later." Abby raised her voice, "What happened, Reverend?"

Mrs Miller gave her husband's hand a little shake.

Like a signal?

"Jonas, dear, tell the police lady what you've just told me."

"Robbers. Thieves." Spittle dripped from the corner of his mouth, but his expression radiated nothing but vague anxiety. "Trying to steal my windows."

"The window was damaged in the hailstorm," Abby said patiently.

The reverend leaned forward, blinking earnestly. "No. No. They were inside the church. Heard them when Florrie and I crossed the road. Heard them knock something over inside. Then they stepped on the broken glass."

"Could you be mistaken? I was in the church only moments ago, and no one was there," Roman said but then he remembered the fallen hymn books.

"I'm not deaf, young man. Someone was inside. Must have heard our voices because they fled out the door and hid in the graveyard." The vicar raised a trembling hand and pointed. "No idea how they got in. We'd locked the place up when we heard on the radio a storm was coming."

Roman leaned close to Abby and said, "It's possible. The church doors were open when I arrived."

"Thanks for that info." Abby addressed the Millers, "Roman will walk you home. You'll both be required to make statements."

"The robber…"

"If there was an intruder, then there'll be evidence in the church. I'll check it out and meet you back at your house."

The police siren cut off and a car door slammed.

"Sounds like help has arrived." Roman ran a hand over his hair.

Abby leaned close and muttered, "Probably Riley. We'll have to do a thorough search for that damn weapon."

"I guess that says goodbye to our dinner?" Roman raised questioning eyebrows.

"Sorry. I have no idea how long I'll be, and the boys must be starving by now." Abby sounded glum.

Roman didn't blame her. From all appearances, it was going to be a long night.

He took her hand in his. "I'll take them over to the pub and get something for you in a takeaway container. Maybe I can bring it to the police station?"

Her lovely smile lit up her face. "Lifesaver."

After kissing his wife's fingertips, much to the old couple's intense interest, Roman assisted Mrs Miller to her feet. Her husband rose and fussed with his dressing gown, pulling it tighter around his frame.

Head high, Mrs Miller marched off, dragging her husband by the arm. "Do hurry, Jonas, before you catch your death of cold."

"Stay warm," Roman warned Abby before following the Millers.

He shook his head as he watched the elderly couple bend their heads and whisper to each other.

No doubt plotting their statements.

He didn't envy Abby's job of trying to get straight answers from that pair, but he hoped the rifle would be found and placed well out of reach of the good Reverend.

Next time, they may not be so lucky.

Next time, someone could be hurt.

CHAPTER 19

Friday morning saw Abby compiling reports from the day before as well as herding the Millers into the station to take their official statements. Despite repeated attempts by both Riley and herself, neither would budge from their initial testimony regarding the gun.

Frustrated, Abby waved them out the door, then, after saying she was taking her lunch break, walked down Willow Drive, and turned the corner onto Mt Ingalls Road. At the post office, she purchased two pre-paid mobile phones for the boys.

When the storm hit, her first thought had been the boys' safety. Now with a mobile each, she'd be able to contact them whenever she needed. And it would put them on a level playing field with other kids their own age. These days, everyone had a mobile.

With her purchases securely in her handbag, she walked on into Main Street to assess the storm damage. When she reached the barricades surrounding the footpath and the front of the IGA store, she was amazed no one had been seriously injured. She spent eight minutes at the Cyprus Café, enjoying a coffee and slice of baklava, before hurrying back to work.

The rest of the day, Abby and her fellow police officers were rushed off their feet, calls for assistance, a false alarm about an intruder (turned out to be a homeowner attempting to gain access to his back window after he lost his keys down a drain), checking on roads, and the list went on. Both she and AJ had examined the church in the bright light of day and taken photos of the broken glass, the front door and the spilled books. They'd also dusted for fingerprints, not expecting to get anywhere with that, and they eventually proved to be right, no distinct prints were found. Together with AJ, Abby also spent a couple of hours doing a grid search of the cemetery for the rifle, again, they came up wanting.

By the time her shift finished, Abby was tired, irritated, and anxious to get home, kick off her shoes, collapse on her new chaise, and put her feet up.

Since AJ was on call that night and would have the paddy wagon, she asked Roman to pick her up outside the chemist as she had a prescription to get filled. She'd only been waiting a minute or so before he rolled up.

With a grateful sigh, she slid into the car and fastened her seatbelt. "What a day."

"Agreed. And, what a night." Roman checked for traffic, before pulling out onto the road. "You looked bushed, hon. But never fear; your cook is here."

She laughed. "Thanks for the lift. Where are Drew and Eddie?"

"At the library." Meeting her astonished stare, Roman

grinned.

"Yeah. I know but apparently there is a girl involved, in the case of Drew, anyway. I believe the lure of borrowing a DVD on horse-riding was the clincher for Eddie."

"Bless them." Smiling, Abby leaned back and closed her eyes. "I bought them mobile phones today."

"You read my mind. I was going to talk to you about that same thing tonight."

Fatigue was tugging her under. She yawned and opened her eyes. Looking at Roman, she asked, "Still busy?"

"Yes. There're a few houses and outbuildings roofs that we haven't been able to get to yet. Minor damage only. They can wait for another day. And I can't tell you the number of fallen trees blocking people's driveways that remain to be cleared. Plus, there's a report of some road up near Craigellachie with numerous downed trees as well. It'll take weeks before Bindarra is back to herself again."

Abby frowned. "Weeks?" Did that mean, he intended to see the job through to the end?

Roman tapped the steering wheel in a fast beat but didn't respond.

"I had a text message about another SES meeting tonight," Abby eventually said.

Nodding, Roman flicked on his indicator, turned right into Church Street, then took the first right again. "It'll be quick. We're asking members to volunteer for the weekend roster. Hopefully, those who were unable to help yesterday and today will step up and give those who've worked the past thirty-six hours a rest."

"I'm sure there'll be plenty of willing helpers."

"I get that same feeling." Roman grinned as he pulled up outside the library. "The meeting should only go for half an hour max, babe, and we'll be on our way home."

Home.

She swallowed. The thought filled her with warmth and comfort. And it had everything to do with the man sitting beside her and the two boys running towards the car.

Until she remembered the email.

And suddenly she didn't want to go home.

※

Dinner a la Roman was fabulous, as it usually was, the man knew his way around a kitchen.

Abby mopped up the last of the gravy on her plate with a piece of gluten-free bread and popped it into her mouth. "You're a good cook, Roman. I don't know how you do it."

"Simple." He waited until she looked over at him before he continued, "Mindfulness. I pay attention to the task at hand. No running around doing four things at once."

"I can't help it. There's always such a lot to remember and do." Abby grimaced.

"There's a solution for that, babe."

"Hmmm." She eyed his innocent expression with suspicion.

Don't think I don't know what you mean!

Deciding that was a loaded comment she had no idea how to answer, she smiled at Drew and Eddie. "Well, since Roman cooked, it's up to us to clean up."

They made a mountain out of their moaning and groaning, but she could tell it was all play-acting. While Abby washed up, the boys dried and cleared away the table, all while filling her ears with their day, what one of their friends said, what another one did, what they both wanted to do this weekend.

She couldn't believe the change in Eddie and Drew. They were revealing more and more of themselves. She loved discovering new things about them, and was touched to her soul at the trust they placed in her.

Since it was Friday night, she'd decreed they could watch a movie of their choosing on Netflix, providing it was suitable for their ages. To her surprise, they picked *'Moana'*, and they all settled down beside the fire.

But before Drew turned the television on, Abby gave him and his brother their new mobile phones, saying they were a gift from both herself and Roman.

To say the brothers were moved by the gesture was an understatement. Drew stammered out a *"thankyou"* while Eddie settled for hugging Abby, then Roman, and then Abby again.

Roman lightened the moment by tussling Eddie's hair and wrestling Drew into a mock-headlock. With a pretend battle yell, Eddie leaped on Roman's back. Laughing, they all tumbled onto the rug where Pinky promptly jumped in, licking any face she could reach.

Smiling, Abby quickly shifted her feet out of the way as they rolled about. She couldn't remember when she'd felt this happy.

After the movie had ended, the boys trailed off to bed. Abby returned from tucking them in to find Roman sitting in the corner of the chaise sketching, under the glow of a floor lamp.

"What are you working on?"

He paused, quirking an eyebrow, a teasing smile playing about his lips.

Heat unfurled in her belly. Needs and longings she'd hoped to keep under wraps, slowly unravelled in her mind.

"Are you certain you want to know?"

She drew a sharp breath. "Actually, no, I don't."

"Then, we'll discuss this later." He shut the book, placing both it and his pencil onto the table. "I need to tell you something important, Abby."

She sank into the comfortable chaise cushions, tensing a little when he rose and moved over to join her.

"The night of the storm and when we were in the cemetery, I want to tell you how proud I am of you. You're a fine police officer, Abby, and the sensitive way you dealt with the Millers was simply beautiful."

"Roman," she whispered, feeling herself melt inside.

"But there's more." He shifted until he faced her. His fingers captured her chin, tilting her face a little and he gazed down at her with an intensity that sent quivers of fire dancing along her veins. "I've never stopped loving you, Abby. I've never stopped wanting you."

"I'm the same, Roman." She searched his eyes, there were no shadows lurking in that clear silver.

"Dance with me."

"There's no music."

"It's in our hearts, babe." Quirking his eyebrows, he murmured, "For old time's sake?" Humming in a liquid baritone, he drew her to her feet.

They swayed together, dipping and gliding around the furniture. Their bodies were attuned in perfect harmony as if they'd never been parted.

Abby was aware of the quiet of the night beyond these walls, the crackle and hiss of the fire, the intimacy of the shadowed room, and the hard strength of his body so close to hers. He moved against her then away, then back again, a languid rhythm that drove her crazy with desire.

Their kiss last night had never left her thoughts. Now it burned in her memory with the promises of more. She knew, regardless of what happened tomorrow, or the day after, she wanted to indulge in the passion they'd shared so long ago.

"Do you think it'll be the same?" She leaned back to watch his expression.

"Sex?" Roman looked thoughtful. "We were good together."

"I know, but what if we've changed?"

"I hope you're not inferring we're too old." His voice sounded aggrieved. "I've heard you can get these little blue pills…"

She chuckled and tapped his nose. "I've always loved that about you."

"What's that, babe?"

"You don't take yourself too seriously."

"The only thing I take seriously…" He looked thoughtful for a second. "No, hang on. The only two things I take seriously is my job, and us."

Fancy bringing up his job! At a moment like this! And he said it first.

Irritation flared. She opened her mouth to berate him

only to catch the laughter in his eyes. "You!" She slapped his chest.

"Abby."

The amusement fled, drowned by the tsunami of hunger blazing in his taut jaw.

Their lips met.

Abby sighed, as he plundered her mouth.

His heart thundered beneath her touch. His chest molten heat through the fabric of his shirt.

She wanted nothing between them.

She wanted them both naked.

She wanted him.

He swept his hands down the length of her body, pressing her closer until she could feel every hard muscle he possessed.

Breathless, her blood pulsating through her veins, she broke the kiss to whisper, "My bed."

"Now, you're talking." He scooped her into his arms, his mouth fused again on hers as if he couldn't bear for them to be apart, and he carried her to her room.

<hr>

"I've got some sketches to show you." Roman flicked on her bedside lamp.

Snuggled up beside him, she kept her eyes shut. "I've heard that one before."

He chuckled. "You'll like these sketches."

"You are so full of it." She smiled and opened her eyes.

"Hon, you're the one that keeps telling me how awesome I am."

"I was being kind."

"Cheeky." He planted a hard kiss to her swollen lips, before pushing back the blankets.

Yawning, she pulled the doona up under her chin, burrowing under its warmth. The air had turned icy cold.

Roman wrapped a blanket around his waist then padded from the bedroom. When he returned a few moments later, he had his sketch book in hand. He settled down beside her and wordlessly handed it to her.

Curious, Abby sat up and opened the first two pages. The design for the chicken coop. She grinned, then turned to the next page, gasped, and stared. Deep inside, she began to tremble, shaking loose the foundations of the wall she'd built around herself five years ago. "They're plans for this house."

"Yes." Roman's voice was eager as he leaned closer, his finger tracing the diagrams. "The building has good bones and a solid construction. This sketch is for an extension on both sides of the house. One room would be a bedroom and the one over here, is a family or sun room. Now, see the kitchen." He turned another page showing various kitchen designs. "I've got several ideas. Plus a few different ways the bathroom could be remodelled. I think solar panels is a must, too. What do you think?"

"Looks … it all looks fabulous." Abby fought to control the excitement bubbling inside as she remembered how they'd renovated their old townhouse. Roman's ideas were extensive, a big commitment in terms of both money and time. "But who's going to do all this work? My skills are limited to hanging a picture on the wall."

"You know who, me."

His words hung in the air for several seconds.

"I don't know," she finally whispered. "Roman, I'm so

confused. Look what happened last time ... and there's this email ..."

Tossing the book aside, he cupped her face in his hands. "Hey, you're crying. What's happened? What did it say?"

"That's just it. Nothing. I haven't read it." Abby gulped.

"Ah, the old Abby-with-her-head-in-the-sand trick," he said tenderly.

She gave a watery giggle. "Stop it. I'm not that bad. It *has* been a busy few days."

"Now that's the truth. Okay, babe. How about we read the email together?"

"Yes, I'd like that." Gently she dislodged his hands and reached for her laptop. "Here it is. It's from the foster agency."

She froze as she opened her email account and read the message. Drew and Eddie were to be sent back to Sydney a week Monday. Unable to speak, she remained staring at the screen, her mind in turmoil.

"Damn. Abby, I thought they'd be here at least four weeks!"

"I know. But it looks like they've found a place that can take them for eight months," she managed to croak.

"And then what? Another move to another foster home? And so on, for their rest of their lives?" Mouth compressed, Roman covered his eyes with his hand.

Abby shut down her laptop, and placed it on the bedside table, wondering at her outward composure. Inside, she was being dismantled piece by piece. Unable to express what she felt. Hell, she didn't know what she felt! There was one big, giant ball of emotions rioting inside her head.

"When will you tell them?" Roman's hand fell to his side, his expression shuttered as he met her gaze.

She plucked at the doona cover for a few seconds, then said, "Not yet."

"Don't leave it to the last minute. They need to be prepared." He glanced away.

She looked down.

His hands were clenched into fists and suddenly, she wanted to bawl her eyes out. "It's good the placement is for eight months. You never know, it could end up being permanent."

He whirled around to face her, his gaze fierce. "They already have a permanent home. All you have to do is say the words, Abby, and we can apply to foster them ourselves."

"It's not that simple." She cracked, covering her face with her hands, heaving dry, racking sobs. "I don't know, Roman. I just don't know."

Roman sighed heavily. His arms came around her, pulling her in close as he kissed the top of her head. "Hush, now, it's okay, babe. We still have a week together. Promise me one thing, though, Abby."

Wiping her eyes, she raised her head.

"Promise you won't shut me out."

"I can do that." She raised her hands around his neck and nestled in close, loving the soft prickle of his chest hairs against her skin.

His breathing hitched. He lowered his head and kissed her, capturing her in a bubble of bliss where only they existed and tomorrow had no meaning.

He was right. They had a week. And Abby intended to make every day count.

CHAPTER 20

"Tuck your elbows in to your sides. Bear down on your feet. Keep your heels down," advised Abby from where she kept a close watch as Eddie mounted on Geronimo, trotted in a tight circle in the paddock next to the house. In one hand, Abby held a lunge line attached to her horse's bridle.

A corral would come in handy right about now, she thought ruefully. "You're doing great, Eddie."

Drew yelled from where he stood near the barn, holding Pinky in his arms. "Yeah. You're a real cowboy."

Beaming, Eddie twisted around to wave at his brother. The reins fell from his hand and immediately, Geronimo broke into a canter. Eddie wobbled in the saddle and for one horrible second, Abby thought he'd fall. But he righted himself, clinging to the pommel, his expression more determined than afraid.

"Easy, boy. Steady." Abby shortened the lunge line and obeying, the big gelding slowed to an amble. "Don't jerk on the reins; use a nice, steady slide to stop him."

Eddie let go of the pommel sufficiently to weave the reins through his fingers and bring Geronimo to a halt.

"Well done." Abby moved closer, running a soothing hand along Geronimo's neck. The big horse snorted in response, shaking his head and making the bridle jingle.

"I was riding, Abby. Did you see that, Drew? I rode a horse." Eddie swivelled to grin at his brother than back to Abby. "Can I have another go?"

Abby smiled at his enthusiasm. "Not today. We've got visitors coming, remember?"

"What about after school? And next weekend?"

Abby laughed. "Okay. I'll see if I can finish work earlier one day this week, and we can get another hour in before it becomes too dark."

"And next weekend," Eddie insisted.

"Sure." But Abby's smile froze. *'Next weekend'* and then the following Monday they'd be gone. "Before you get yourself cleaned up, you have to help rub Geronimo down."

"Should I put his horse rug on, Abby?" Eddie frowned at the sky, then kicking free from the stirrups, scrambled from the horse.

"We need to work on your technique in dismounting," Abby said wryly. "We can leave it off for a while and say, about three-thirty rug him up for the night."

"Gotcha." Eddie took the reins and began to lead the horse back to the barn. "Hey, Drew. You can have a turn next time."

"I guess I could have a go. Bet I learn to ride before you do, though." Drew gave his brother a playful shove as he walked inside.

"Ha. As if. I'm a natural, aren't I, Abby?"

Abby chuckled. "You're a quick study, I'll say that much. But there's a lot to learn, and it's not only about how to ride. You need to learn about caring for your mount also."

Looking thoughtful, Eddie began to uncinch the girth straps. "I'd like that."

Abby showed the boy where to stow the saddle and how to rub the horse down, before removing Geronimo's bridle. She gave the horse an apple and one final pat on the nose. Together, with Eddie on one side and Drew, still holding Pinky, on the other, she left the barn. When they reached the house, Drew set the little dog onto the ground.

Abby walked up the steps and opened the door. "Put your smelly clothes in the dirty clothes basket please, Eddie."

"Okay, Abby," he sang out before running down the hall.

"Want me to help with anything?" Drew shoved his hands into his jeans pockets.

"How about you get the trestle table and the camp chairs from the garden shed?" Abby said with a smile.

"No worries." He whistled for Pinky to follow and left the house again.

Abby strolled into the kitchen to come up short. "Oh my …! Roman, how many people are we feeding today?" Her gaze studied the table, loaded with food.

His smile brighter than gold, he grinned over his shoulder as he stirred the contents of a pot on the stove. "Want this to be a good day for the boys to remember." He grimaced. "I guess for all of us."

"They'll certainly remember the food. There's so much

of it." She sniffed the air. "Wow, that smells like my favourite, roasted vegetables."

"Got it in one." Roman bent down and opened the door.

Inhaling the sudden rush of garlic, roasted onions, and winter vegetables, and melted cheese, Abby could have died on the spot. Her tummy rumbled as Roman laid the baking dish onto a wooden chopping board on the sink.

"I've got two trays of these." Roman tested a vegetable with a fork. "Plus, there's potato bake, a garden salad, a Caesar salad, a trifle, and herbed bread. Then for the barbeque, there's the beef sausages, lamb and rosemary rissoles and rump steak."

He sounded worried.

Hiding her amusement, Abby hugged him from behind. "Don't stress. I'm sure there'll be enough food. And if there're any leftovers, we can have them through the week. I can man the barbeque since you've done all this work."

He turned around in her arms, not bothering to hide his wince. "No thanks; I've seen your work. You know I enjoy the cooking side of things."

Abby smiled as she leaned in for a kiss. "Looks like I'm the clean-up crew."

"You got it, babe."

"They're here!" hollered Eddie from the other end of the house. He came pelting into the room.

"Socks then shoes, Eddie, before you go outside." Abby pointed to his feet.

Rolling his eyes, he disappeared back down the hall.

Abby washed her hands in the sink, drying them with the towel Roman handed her. She drew a deep breath and met his eyes. He looked as nervous as she felt. "Here we go."

He nodded and together they went to the front door to greet their guests.

A white Toyota Prada was parked in front of their house, and two boys piled from the back seat.

"Ethan! Noah! Over here!" called Drew from where he was unfolding a camp chair at the side of the house.

As the two boys raced off, their parents emerged.

Abby and Roman walked down the steps to greet them.

"Bing Beasley," said a man in his late thirties as he extended his hand to Roman. "This is the missus, Hester. And we've given Noah's mum, Natalie, a lift."

Roman introduced himself and Abby and after handshakes and smiles all round, Abby suggested they adjourn to under a large lilly pilly tree where the boys were clowning around with the camp chairs.

"We've got an esky and some tucker. And we've brought chairs." Bing gestured over his shoulder at his car.

Roman stepped forward. "I'll give you a hand."

Another vehicle rolled up the drive, Marsha and Chen Wang with their son, Gavin.

It wasn't long before everyone was settled under the tree. To Abby's surprise, the day went smoothly. The parents were friendly and seemed happy to meet new people. Roman cooked up a wonderful meal, and the women were, frankly, envious of his skills.

"Bing couldn't boil an egg to save himself," Hester Beasley said as she tucked into a medium-rare steak.

Natalie helped herself to another serving of salad. "I'm lucky in that there's only the two of us. Noah is easy to please, food wise, like me. This food is deelish, Abby. I want to save room for dessert, but potato bake is one of my weaknesses."

"I'm the same, Natalie." Abby smiled. "I'm not fussy with food either, but I love Roman's cooking."

"I wish I could say the same." Marsha toasted her husband, where he stood around the barbeque with Roman and Bing, with her mug of hot tea. "Chen has been known to cook me breakfast in bed on Mother's Day."

"And how was it?" Hester leaned forward.

"Bearable. Just."

And they all laughed.

To Abby's relief no one questioned her and Roman's relationship and no-one questioned their relationship with the boys'. She guessed the rumour mill had already done its rounds about town and to her surprise, she began to relax and enjoy the easy company. They accepted her, Roman, and the boys at face value.

She chewed a mouthful of Roman's roasted cheesy vegetables, savouring the combination of flavours on her tongue, and gazed at Drew and Eddie kicking a football around the paddock with their friends. Pinky yapped hysterically under their feet, but the boys were careful where they kicked the ball.

Faces flushed with exertion, eyes sparkling, yelling and laughing with their mates, they were a far cry from the orphaned boys who'd landed on her doorstep mere days ago.

Her eyes misted as Drew picked up Pinky and popped her inside his jacket. To give her a breather? Or keep her out of the way for a while? Either way, it didn't matter. His action showed a level of responsibility she'd never thought him capable of that first night they'd met. He was the one responsible for bringing all these people here together. He was the one responsible for making her feel like she really was a part of Bindarra Creek.

I'm going to miss him.
I'm going to miss them both.

ROMAN STOOD on the front verandah, his arm firmly around Abby's waist as they waved their guests goodbye. "That was a good day, babe."

He leaned in closer and nuzzled her neck, then trailed his mouth over her soft skin. Feeling her give that little jolt of awareness under his touch, he smiled.

"I had fun."

"We all did." Roman placed his hands on her shoulders and gently turned her so she faced where Drew and Eddie were carrying the trestle table from the paddock back to the small lawn locker. "The Beasleys are keen to return the favour the next time Bing is back in town. Apparently, he works in a mine near Blackwater as a mechanic."

"A fly-in, fly-out kind of guy? You've got that in common then." Abby smiled.

Pulling her closer, Roman rested his cheek on hers. "Chen's interested in boxing and wants Gavin to learn as well."

"Another point in common, although I know you haven't checked out the new boxing ring as yet." Abby sighed, her body relaxing against his. "Hester is in the local book club and has invited Marsha, Natalie and me to join."

"That's good. You used to love reading crime novels."

"True. I'm thinking about it."

"Everyone wants to go kayaking in the National Park. Make it a kind of joint family affair." His gaze followed the boys as they staggered to the shed with a load of chairs. The kids were laughing and teasing each other.

I'm going to miss them.

She stepped away and, taking his hands in hers, looked at him. "We were like a family today, weren't we, Roman?"

"Yeah, babe. We were."

Closing her eyes, she whispered, "I wonder if they'll still want to know me after the boys have gone."

Squeezing his own eyes shut against the sudden twist in his gut, he forced out, "Hard to say. And it's not Monday yet. I want you to remember today, Abby."

Abby released her grip on his hands and turned to walk down the steps. "I don't think I'll ever forget."

CHAPTER 21

*A*fter dropping the boys off at school, Abby was smiling when she entered the police station the following Tuesday. Roman was still living in her home, much to the boys' delight.

And don't forget my delight, she admonished herself. Since Sunday, she'd kept debating whether she should ask him to check out of Fig Tree Lodge and stay with her for the remainder of his time in Bindarra Creek.

She couldn't deny waking up beside him was simply wonderful.

And for today, that was enough.

Shrugging off her jacket, she slung it over the back of her chair. Riley nodded and she greeted him before starting work and finishing an outstanding report on a fender-bender of the day before. The past few days had been busy with the town rallying together in the aftermath of the hailstorm but despite the damage inflicted, morale remained high.

The front door swung open with a crash. She smiled at

AJ as he bustled inside bearing coffees from the Cyprus Café.

"You're a mind reader! Thanks, AJ."

"No worries, Senior Constable," AJ said with a cheeky wink. "Anything happening?"

"Wasn't that hailstorm enough for you?"

AJ handed out the coffees. "No way. I need drama. I need action!"

Abby laughed and took the lid off the cardboard cup. She took a sip and sighed. "Stavros gets it perfect every time."

"You look like you're in a good mood. Again." Smirking, AJ took his seat and spun himself around and around in his chair. "What do you think, Sarge?"

"I noticed." Senior Sergeant grinned, then toasted Abby with his cup. "Care to share?"

Abby enunciated slowly, "No. Way."

"Damn." After swallowing a few mouthfuls of coffee, Riley wiped his mouth with the back of his hand. "Listen up. I want a drive through town this morning and another late in the arvo. Keep an eye out for any idiots who may decide looting is their new vocation. Plus, the hoardings over the front of the IGA store will need to be checked that they're still intact."

He held up a hand as Abby opened her mouth to speak. "I know your hubby has organised the SES to inspect all the temporary protections on a daily basis. But a constant visible police presence walking and driving through the streets will make people feel more at ease."

AJ nodded as he scribbled on a pad.

Abby looked up from her computer screen. "Any idea when the Westburys will have the damage repaired?"

"No. According to Bob, the insurance assessor has yet to set foot in town. But at least the remainder of the building has been declared safe. Roman has the front boarded off to restrict access from both inside and outside. That was a good move for the Westburys." Riley gave an approving smile at Abby. "It means, they're still in business and can operate from the rear of the shop."

"The entire roof could have caved in Sarge. My Mum was inside, doing her grocery shop." AJ's eyes widened.

"We were lucky no one was seriously injured," agreed Riley.

Abby moved onto the remaining item on her list. "What about the caravan park? Have you heard whether power has been restored?"

"Haven't been given an update. As of late yesterday, the park's two downed power poles had yet to be repaired and were still marked with tiger tails," Riley said. "I did see an Ausgrid vehicle parked alongside the substation this morning, though."

"Poor buggers if it's still on the blink. I would like to do a run out to the park this morning, Sarge. Do a walk-through and have a chat to anyone who appears to be struggling." Abby typed in a note on her keyboard.

"Good idea, Abby. If there is, put them in touch with the CWA ladies. I'll put a call in and see if I can rattle some cages and get the work done ASAP. The good news is, that's the last remaining power issue we have in town."

Abby gave a wry smile. "Which only leaves damaged roofs and houses."

"Don't forget the church window." Sarge pointed his pen at her.

"Poor Reverend Miller." Abby sighed. "He was very upset."

"He's damn lucky we didn't run him in for firing off that bloody gun," grumbled Riley. "Call on Mrs Miller again while you're out and about, Abby. Encourage her to get her husband assessed by a doctor. I want to know that weapon is secured somewhere he can't find it. We can't allow a repeat of last Thursday night. He could have shot someone."

"Will do, Sarge." She checked the time, then logged off her computer. "I'll head out now and make the vicarage my first call."

Riley waved her on her way.

After saying goodbye to AJ who was off to do a beat on foot, Abby left the station and crossed to the paddy wagon.

When she pulled up outside the vicarage, she took a moment to collect her thoughts and decide how she'd approach this tricky situation. Advising a woman her husband needed to seek medical attention wasn't easy when the woman didn't want to listen. So far, nothing in the way Mrs Miller had acted had given Abby any reason to believe she'd be amenable to the idea.

Someone rapped against her window.

Automatically, Abby's hand went to her holster. Heart thumping, she turned to find Edwina Lette and her pal, Pamela Brown, standing beside the police car.

Making a series of grimacing faces, Edwina pounded on the window again.

Abby motioned for them to step aside and when they obeyed, she opened the door. Reaching inside, she grabbed her jacket and shrugged it over her vest before zippering it up. "Good morning, ladies. What can I do for you?"

"It's what we can do for you." Bundled up in a hot-pink puffer jacket, white leggings and pink gumboots, Edwina looked like an overblown marshmallow.

In contrast, her partner-in-crime wore a knee-length, black trench coat that hung from her angular shoulders making her appear thinner than usual. A grey and green woolly hat, much like a teapot cosy, was rammed over her hair, and the tip of Pamela's nose was red from the cold. She sniffled, then pulled a purple handkerchief from her pocket.

Edwina danced sideways, flapping a hand. "Keep your germs to yourself, Pam."

"I don't have a cold. It's the wind chill." Pamela blew her nose vigorously.

Closing the door behind her, Abby gazed over at the vicarage where a bright blue tarp still covered a portion of the roof. "Are you visiting, Mrs Miller?"

"Kinda. We've been waiting for you."

"Really? How did you know I was coming?"

Edwina touched the side of her nose and winked. "We didn't but we know you've checked the cemetery and the church. And had the Millers in the police station for their statements. But we know Florrie. She can be stubborn."

Abby hesitated, aware of her audience's breathless anticipation of what she'd say next. "I can't comment on an on-going investigation."

Edwina cackled and elbowed her buddy. "Told you so, Pam. Well, let's get moving. Been sitting on a bloody cold tombstone for so long my bum is numb."

Abby switched her glance to the cemetery and shivered, remembering how the icy wind had howled through the pine trees in an eerie moan.

Her expression crafty, Edwina rattled on, "We were visiting Pam's family."

Blank, Abby said, "Huh?"

"Pam's husband and son." The old woman jerked her head to the side. "In the cemetery."

"Oh, I see. I'm very sorry for your loss, Mrs Brown."

"Call her Pam. We're all one big family here in BC." Edwina drew a leather pouch from a large crocheted bag and slipped a rolled smoke between her lips. Ignoring her friend's irritated hiss, she flicked a lighter, before stuffing her pouch and lighter back into the bag. She sucked down hard on the smoke then, head back, blew a slow steady stream of smoke into the air.

Abby caught the sweet scent instantly. "Is that …?"

Eyes as bright as a magpie's, Edwina smirked. "Medicinal. I allow myself one smoke a week. Grow it myself behind the old stables."

It's not worth the paperwork.

Jamming her cold hands into her jacket pocket, Abby began to walk towards the house. The two old ladies fell into step, flanking her either side.

Probably making sure I don't do a run for it.

"I see your hubby's moved into your home. Your skin is glowing."

Abby rolled her eyes as said skin turned red hot.

Edwina continued in a gleeful tone, "Nothing like solid sex to keep you young and fit. Why, only last week, I had a very interesting meeting with …"

"The senior constable doesn't want to hear about your love life, Edwina."

Abby gave mental thanks for Pamela's swift interjection.

"Pity. But at least I have a life. Although, you could if you wanted to, Pam." Edwina took another puff on her smoke.

"If you're referring to Roy Towns, then don't waste your breath. There is nothing between us," snapped Pamela.

"Poppycock. I've got eyes and ears and can sniff out a romance quicker than a brown snake nabs a frog." Edwina began to sniff the air in loud snorts.

Snuffing out her laughter, Abby wondered how on earth she could make her escape.

Edwina began to hum the wedding march.

Pamela grasped Abby under the elbow and all but dragged her towards the vicarage front door. In a stage whisper, she said, "We're here to help you."

As if on cue, the door opened and there stood Mrs Miller, arms folded tight about her waist, her kind face set in determined lines.

Putting on an extra spurt of speed, Edwina popped up on Abby's other side. "Tea, Florrie? We're freezing. Been visiting the cemetery." She motioned to Pamela as she tossed the butt of her smoke onto the ground where she crushed it under her gumboot.

The sternness dissolved from Florrie's face as she gazed at her friend. "Of course. I should have remembered the date, Pam dear. Come into the kitchen where it's warmer and I'll put the kettle on."

Settled at the scarred timber table and inhaling the scent of a fresh chocolate cake, Abby relaxed. These old ladies might be on the crazy side, but they knew what they were doing. Within minutes, they had Florrie seated, a steaming pot of tea and the cake on the table. They handed around cups, milk, and plates.

Lifting her chin, Florrie looked at Abby squarely. "There's no need to worry, Abby. I've already given my rifle to Edwina for safe keeping."

Abby tried not to wince.

"You know why the senior constable is here, Florrie." Edwina's voice, soft and kind, cut straight to the point. "It can't go on like this. Jonas needs help."

"He'll lose the parish. It's the world to him." Florrie folded as she twisted a tissue between her fingers. Tears filled her eyes and spilled down her cheeks.

"Not necessarily. There's wonderful medication available these days. In a few days or weeks, he could be back to his old self again. And in the meantime, you're more than qualified to step in his shoes. We all know that you trained, even if you've never been officially ordained." Pamela reached over and patted her friend's hand.

Edwina chimed in, "You've given up when we've only begun to fight. We're here, Florrie. Right by your side. And we'll never leave you alone."

Damn. Abby felt the burn of her own tears. She swallowed and was about to speak when Florrie beat her to it.

Dabbing at her wet cheeks, the vicar's wife said, "You're right. I've been a fool, pretending nothing was wrong." Her lips trembled for a second before they firmed. "Can you drive us to the doctor's surgery, Abby?"

"Of course. Make the appointment and let me know."

Edwina smirked. "No need. Already done. We've got Jonas booked in for two-thirty today."

"Oh, Edwina. How did you manage to do that?" Florrie gaped at the other woman.

"Simple. I pretended I was you," Edwina said in a smug tone. "I always wanted to be an actress."

Grinning, Abby checked the time before pouring the tea. "Not a problem, then. After a quick cuppa, I'll head to the caravan park. I'll be back in time to drive you and your husband to the doctor's, Mrs Miller."

"Bless you, dear. I know I lied to you the last time we met and I'm sorry for it. I've been that worried." Florrie blew her nose.

"I understand. I would be just as protective of my husband as you are of yours."

Edwina sliced a small portion of chocolate cake and popped it into her mouth. "See what you're missing, Pam? You can't beat a solid love life. Ask Abby here, she'll tell you I'm right."

And as every eye turned towards her, Abby wished she could melt into the floor.

CHAPTER 22

Mindful of time ticking past, Abby drove into the caravan park and pulled up outside the manager's van. She noted there was an SES utility parked over near the amenities block and wondered who was here. At the notion it could be Roman, her pulse fluttered, and she had to resist the temptation to smear lipstick over her lips. She settled for lip balm.

Pulling on a pair of gloves, she left the car and rapped on the caravan door. She explained to the manager she wanted to talk to the residents and see if further help was required. About to head out the door himself, he waved her on her way.

Several of the park's residents expressed relief when Abby mentioned the CWA hall was open every day that week with plenty of free non-perishable provisions available. Most seemed simply grateful for her presence. Those keen to partake of the hot tea, coffee, and cake that the

CWA ladies would have on the ready, hot-footed it down Court Road.

The two downed power poles were in separate sections of the park. One was close to the amenities block, and Abby decided to check it out first. Even though the electricity wasn't live, the pole had been sectioned off from curious on-lookers by water-filled interlocking yellow polyethylene barriers. She was glad to see no one had disturbed the barricade.

A woman emerged from the amenities block, bucket in one hand, mop in the other.

Glancing up, Abby recognised Natalie Wasson and walked over to greet her. "Hey, Natalie. Great to see you again."

The other woman grinned. "Likewise. Could have been at a better time though. I've been cleaning up a clogged toilet that had leaked all over the floor. Hope I don't stink."

Eyeing the bucket full of murky brown water, Abby took a cautious step backwards. "Sounds like fun. Not."

Natalie laughed. "Noah had a great time on Sunday. Thank you for inviting us."

"It was our pleasure." Abby hesitated, knowing the right answer was, *'let's do it again'* but the words stuck in her throat as she recalled the boys' brief interlude in her life was drawing to a close.

Unless I take them on. Unless <u>we</u> take them on.

Roman and me, together.

Natalie gave a gentle cough making Abby realise she'd been standing like a dumbstruck goose for a good full minute.

Attempting to ignore the other woman's curious stare, she straightened and sought frantically for something to say. "Um, apart from the toilet, any other problems?"

"Power would be good."

"They're working on it," Abby assured her.

"Well, I think there's someone living in their car down by the riverbank." Natalie gave a jerk of her chin to indicate the direction. "I could be wrong of course as I've only seen them once when the car door was open. It was a woman and she was sitting on the back seat with a blanket over her. The car's been in the same spot for about two weeks now and hasn't moved as far as I can tell."

"Really?" Abby gazed towards the river, but the land sloped downwards and with the plethora of caravans and annexes, not to mention the trees that dotted the park, she was unable to see the vehicle. "Thanks. That's good to know. I'll check it out."

Natalie smiled. "Your husband might be there. When I saw him earlier, I told him the same thing."

"Roman's here?"

"Yes, with a couple of other SES blokes. I think they were helping out a middle-aged couple whose annex had ripped and tangled itself over a few of their windows."

Abby nodded.

"I better get back to work. Another hour and I'm finished for the day."

"Thanks again, Natalie. Have a good one." Abby smiled, then headed for the river.

A low fence of treated pine logs was all that separated the edge of the park from the verge of the riverbank.

Abby jumped over the fence and rounded a prickly-leaved shrub, then spotted the car Natalie had mentioned. It was an old 1960s era Volkswagen, and only the front end was visible through a wall of drooping, wattle tree branches.

Abby started down the slope, waving when Roman appeared around the side of the wattle tree. He appeared to be escorting a woman with short, messy black hair, who was lugging a bulging duffle bag.

Crossing the sand to meet him, Abby realised the car was a mere four metres from the water's edge. "Roman. Who have you got here?"

He smiled and gave a salute. "Abby, meet Sara Pyeon."

"Hi, Sara." Abby smiled as she reached their sides.

The other woman gave a short nod, her dark, hooded mono-lid eye shape proclaiming her South Korean heritage.

"Her car broke down and she was unable to move it," Roman added.

After a glance at the partially hidden car, Abby said, "Have you been here long?"

Sara shrugged. "A couple of weeks."

"Visiting family? Friends?" Abby probed, while thinking that was a long time to have a broken-down car in one place.

"I ... I used to know someone who lives in Bindarra and I had nowhere else to go."

"I see. Well, I'm sure Roman has told you that you can't continue to live in your car, especially as it's parked so close to the river."

The other woman ducked her head and chewed her lip.

Frowning, Roman rubbed his chin. "Hang on. Sara. Of course." He snapped his fingers causing Abby and Sara to look at him in surprise. "Do you know a bloke called Dodge? Runs an antique and restoration shop here."

"That sounds like Dodge Myers." A smile broke over Sara's face, vanishing her sullenness.

"Then you must be his former partner from when he was a cop in Sydney." Roman beamed.

Sara's smile withered. "Maybe. What did he say about me?"

"Only that he thought he'd seen you in town," Roman said smoothly.

So smoothly that Abby's internal antenna quivered. "How about we go for a coffee, Sara, and discuss some options for you?"

As the other woman hesitated, Abby continued, "The CWA ladies are serving free hot drinks and cake all day. The hall isn't far. We can even walk it and if you like, we'll leave your bag in the park manager's van. I'm sure he won't mind."

"Excellent, Abby." Roman pulled out his mobile. "How about I ring Dodge? He'll probably want to tag along. He isn't far; actually he's helping fix some poor bloke's annex in the park."

Sara's shoulders seemed to sag. "Okay. But he may not want to see me."

"No harm in asking." Roman stepped aside to make his call.

Sara took a deep breath and met Abby's gaze. "It was me in the church on the night of the storm. I was frightened and wanted something more solid than a car roof over my head."

"Makes sense." Abby nodded. "How did you get inside?"

"I broke the lock." Sara gave a hesitant smile. "After the hail stopped, I was about to leave when someone came through the door threatening to shoot me. I managed to circle around them, run outside and into the cemetery. When I heard a shot, I kept running until I was back in my car."

One mystery solved.

"Would you recognise this person again?"

"No. Sorry. It was too dark."

"Hmmm. Do you by any chance go for walks around the church at night?"

"Sometimes." Looking tired, Sara rubbed her forehead. After a long searching glance at Abby, she shrugged as if coming to a decision. "Hell! What does it matter? My parents died two years ago. Being in the church makes me feel closer to them."

Then Reverend Miller wasn't delusional when he thought someone had been poking about his precious church.

Abby asked, "But why only at night?"

The other woman bit her lip. "I guess I didn't want anyone to notice me."

There's more to her story, but it can wait. The poor thing seems exhausted.

"Come on. I could do with a cuppa and cake." Smiling in a friendly fashion, Abby hooked her arm through Sara's and towed her up the slope and through the caravan park.

Behind them, she heard Roman muttering on his phone as he followed, and when they neared the manager's van, she wasn't surprised to see Dodge Myers loitering beside the door.

"Sara!" A big smile on his face, he bounded towards them.

Abby relinquished her hold as he reached them.

Dodge hauled Sara in close for a hug. "Good to see you, mate. Why didn't you call and tell me you were in town?"

Pulling away, Sara looked ready to burst into tears. She wiped her hand under her nose.

"No biggie." Dodge nudged her shoulder. "I'm just glad to see you. You turning up right now is a stroke of luck. I need someone to give me a hand in the shop. With the damage from the storm last Thursday, I've got my hands full. Think you can take it on? I'll pay you of course."

He rubbed his hands together in a way that reminded Abby of his grandmother. "Won't be much but you'll be able to get on your feet. And be doing me a big favour."

"Are you sure?" A dazed expression crossed Sara's face.

"Hey. I'm positive. I couldn't help you last time, but here and now, I can."

I wonder what happened.

Abby bit back her curiosity as she met Roman's satisfied gaze. He nodded as if to say *'Tell you later.'* "We're off to have coffee at the CWA hall."

Roman gave an easy smile. "I reckon we could all do with a break. I'll tell the other blokes and we'll go together."

"Come on, mate." Dodge took Sara's bag from her. "I'll stow this somewhere safe, first. We've got a lot of catching up to do."

Before striding off with Sara's bag, Dodge mouthed *'thank you'* to Roman from behind Sara's back.

Smiling, Roman moved closer to Abby, then brushed her cheek with his lips. "Meet you two ladies there in ten."

He lowered his voice and added, "Small towns. Aren't they great?"

CHAPTER 23

The following morning, Abby was musing over the wonderful night she'd spent in Roman's arms while she half-heartedly dealt with more paperwork at her desk in the police station. His touch retained the power to float her to the stars, and his kisses soared her to heaven. And no matter how hard she tried, sneaky daydreams of spending the rest of her life with him kept creeping into her thoughts.

Could she try again?

Or would their marriage be forever poisoned by the grief of their shared past?

And what of Drew and Eddie?

Another five days, and they'd be gone. Returned to a new foster home but at least this one held the promise of more than a few weeks.

Scowling, Abby thumped out a sentence on her keyboard.

What if they weren't happy there? What if the family treated them unkindly? Cruelly? Or even if they were indifferent to the boys' wants and needs, and never giving them the love they craved?

She could imagine their loneliness and their hurt. She could imagine how Drew would harden, burying the yearnings in his heart, and how Eddie would turn fearful, his anxiety issues taking hold. In a few years, they could both be emotional messes.

What makes me think, I can do better?

Even with Roman?

Chewing her lower lip, she banged out another line, then squinted at the screen. She rolled her eyes and hit the delete button.

Focus, Abby, or you'll be here a month of Sundays filling out this report.

The front door opened.

Looking up, she pasted a smile on her face when she recognised the dark-haired young man entering the building as Grady Flannigan, another SES volunteer and a local farmer.

He rushed to the front counter where he began to tap an impatient finger. With AJ and Riley out on patrol, Abby was *'it'* for the next hour or so.

Wheeling back her chair, she rose from her desk and crossed the room. "Grady. What can I do for you?"

"Hi, Abby. I've got a problem."

Abby walked around the counter and drew a notepad towards her. Picking up her pen, she said, "Okay, fire away."

"The water in my dam is contaminated."

She paused. "Are you sure?"

He nodded, saying harshly, "Yep. We found three dead sheep on the sides of the dam. No signs they'd been savaged by wild dogs. We fenced the area off in case there was something wrong with the water, then Opal had a sample tested yesterday when she was in Armidale. She emailed the results to me last night."

Abby remembered meeting his fiancée, Opal, a few times at SES training nights. The young woman had struck Abby as being confident and practical. Hardly someone who'd make a false claim. "Did you bring a copy of the report?"

"Downloaded it." Grady handed over a USB stick.

"Thanks. This may help to narrow down the source."

"What if it's not a natural cause?"

Frowning, Abby considered the young farmer. Not wanting to put words in his mouth, she said, "I think you should explain that comment."

Grady shoved a hand through his hair. "I bumped into Damien Forster in High Street this morning. He reckons he's got a couple of sick cows on his property and it could be connected to my dead sheep."

Abby raised her eyebrows. "I heard Mr Forster isn't that knowledgeable about farm life. I thought he worked as a handyman in town."

"True. But I'm only repeating what he told me." Grady hunched his shoulders. "Either way. My water supply is stuffed, and I can't use it on my crops." He pushed the USB closer to Abby.

"I'll look into it. What are you going to do?"

He grimaced. "We'll have to truck in water, I guess. Opal's job will help tide us over, but it's going to be tough. I've got no idea how to fix the contamination, though."

"I'm sorry." Abby fingered the USB stick. "Let's hope this is an isolated incident and it doesn't spread elsewhere. Please contact the station, if anything further happens. We'll be sure to keep you in the loop, too."

After Grady left, she plugged in the data stick. As she read the report, her heart sank to the bottom of her police-issued boots. The test had revealed the presence of melioidosis which could be fatal to both humans and animals alike. But what it didn't say was to what extent the water was contaminated. Abby suspected further tests would have to be done and, in the meantime, they'd have to somehow discover what had caused the problem. And, if possible, how to make it go away.

Go away.

The words made her think of Drew and Eddie, and how fast the days were flying by.

Soon they'd be gone from her life forever.

And she had yet to break the news to them.

Every night, she'd look at them seated around her dining table, chatting about their day and joking with Roman, and think it was time they knew the truth. And every night she choked on the words not wanting to ruin these last, precious days.

I have to tell them. And soon.

With dismay, she realised her hands were trembling and there were tears on her cheeks. She pulled herself together. There was work to be done. She logged her report and decided after AJ and Riley returned, she'd do a drive through town hoping to have a chat with Damian if she could find him.

And keep an eye out for that car.

Forty minutes later, she was cruising along Main Street when quite unexpectedly, she spotted the car that had been eluding her for the past two weeks.

There it was!

The Lexus convertible.

Parked outside the chemist on Main Street in full view.

Innocent? Or hiding in plain sight?

Stunned, Abby pulled in behind it and radioed AJ to run the number plates. While she waited, she carefully scanned what she could see of the interior.

No sign of the driver.

She turned her attention to the footpath where the locals wandered about their daily business. Ryan Rossiter strolled by, a length of four-by-two balanced on his shoulder. Dulcie Stirling stalked past, holding a string bag of vegetables, talking nineteen to the dozen to Kel Jones, the fire captain. Poor Kel wore a trapped expression. He rolled his eyes at Abby. Across the road, Maureen Molyneux was loading her car with a crate of seedlings.

Nothing out of the ordinary.

Just another day in Bindarra Creek.

When AJ came back on the radio, he advised the car was owned by a Fatima Maloof and hadn't been reported stolen. Abby asked him to do a background check on the owner and call her with the results ASAP. Thoughtfully, she tapped in the details on her mini iPad before placing the device on the seat.

Taking a deep breath, she stepped onto the footpath, shutting the paddy wagon's door behind her. Her heart rate picked up speed as she approached the other vehicle. Finally, she may have some answers. Bending down she checked inside, back seat was clear, nothing in the front passenger side. She straightened, running a hand over the dents on the roof that appeared to have been caused by hail. So, the car had been in town that day.

Where?

And what had the driver been doing during the storm?

She touched the bonnet. Engine was still warm so the driver couldn't be far.

Pushing a stray strand of hair behind her ear, she was about to walk back to the police wagon when her attention was caught by a short-statured woman emerging onto the footpath from a nearby shop. The woman wore a pink and pale blue floral Hijab, and black trousers under her blue tunic.

Fatima Maloof, AJ had said.

Abby would eat her hat if the woman coming towards her wasn't her quarry.

CHAPTER 24

What with the contaminated dam and the after-effects of the hailstorm still being felt in the town, Abby worked late that night. She'd had no time to reflect or process what had happened. The meeting with Fatima Maloof was like a tape on re-play over and over inside her mind, driving her crazy with unanswered questions. It wasn't until after dinner that she had a chance to speak to Roman.

She'd done her best to act normal, like nothing was wrong but the boys must have picked up on the violent emotions churning inside her. They bickered and tormented each other all through the lasagne perfectly cooked by Roman, then whined and moaned while they helped clear up.

And Roman had kept throwing her questioning glances with that way he had of his, of raising his eyebrows and tilting his head a trifle to the left.

Whereas before she'd always found it endearing – tonight, it added to her aggravation.

Motioning for Roman to follow her outside, Abby left the house and stalked towards to the chicken coop. Geronimo poked his head over the fence and snickered. She paused and gave him a pat, but the feel of his tough hide under her hand and his faint horsey smell failed to soothe her.

She doubted nothing could ever soothe her again.

Betrayal was like a red mist inside her head.

"What's going on Abby? You've look like you're about to explode. Is it the boys? I think we need to tell them sooner rather than later, their days here are numbered."

Abby kept marching towards the coop where she turned to face him. "Why say it like that?"

"Because it's true. They're happy here. We're all happy here."

"I can't believe you're saying this, now. After what happened."

"Damn it, Abby. What did happen?"

"She lied to me. I had a feeling she was holding something back. But this! This is too much." Her voice vibrated with an anger that seemed to hum in the cold, night air.

"Abby, please. Tell me what's wrong." Roman ran his hands up and down her arms.

Jaw tight, she shook off his touch. "Were you in on this?"

"In on what?" Roman sucked in an exasperated breath. "For heaven's sake, Abby, you need to be more specific." He waved a hand towards the house. "Dragging me off in this clandestine fashion. The boys will be wondering what the hell is going on."

"They're not the only ones!"

The silver in Roman's eyes turned stormy. His jaw tightened.

Unable to keep still, Abby paced away from him to the other side of the coop. Roman's breath was hot on the back of her neck.

Whirling around, she confronted him, slapping her mobile against her open palm. "I located the car. And its driver."

The anger left as his face paled. "My God, Abby. Did he threaten you?" He shot a quick glance towards the house where the light on the back verandah spilled over the steps. Looking momentarily puzzled, he examined the area surrounding the house and what he could see of the front drive.

Abby tracked his gaze.

Nothing moved.

Not far from where they stood, a lone owl hooted, causing her to flinch.

"This isn't like you. Did he try to hurt you?" Roman gripped her shoulders, pulling her closer.

Abby willed herself to remain stiff and not to fold into his protective touch. "Nothing like that happened. He is a she. The driver is an innocent member of the public. A dentist, recently widowed, who's been staying in a hotel in Tamworth. She's considering moving her kids and elderly mum to the country. She's been driving around and inspecting properties for sale in the Tamworth and Bindarra Creek areas."

Suddenly, she felt incredibly tired and pressed the back of her hand over her eyes.

"I don't understand. I can't see anything in what you've

told me that could be a threat. Maybe there's another Lexus getting around town," Roman muttered.

"I doubt it. I think I've got a good idea what's going on. The woman's name is Dr Fatima Maloof. Ring any bells?"

Roman shook his head. "I've never heard of her. Should I?"

"You tell me." Abby pushed his hands from her shoulders and scrolled through her contacts.

"Who are you calling?"

"Elizabeth." Abby dialled. "She's the one who told me the boys were in danger. She's the one who phoned you supposedly saying *I* was in danger."

"I still have no idea what you're talking about," muttered Roman, clearly irritated. Then his brow cleared. "Unless…"

Abby shushed him with a savage slash of her hand through the air.

The phone rang and rang before switching to an answering machine. Abby fought to keep her voice even. "Elizabeth, I know you're listening. Please pick up the phone. I'm not going to stop calling until you answer."

Her fingers clenched tighter around her mobile as she waited.

No response.

She tried again, and this time Elizabeth picked up.

"Abby, how lovely to hear your voice. How are the boys?" Elizabeth sounded as if she hadn't a care in the world.

Gritting her teeth, Abby snapped, "They're fine. We need to talk."

"I do dislike hearing those words."

"I bet." Abby gave a short laugh. Beside her Roman

shook his head in disbelief then motioned for her to continue. "I'm placing you on speaker."

"Then that must be Roman with you. Still. How wonderful."

"Hi, Elizabeth. I would have thought you would have contacted us before now. Checking on the boys' welfare, and so on," Roman said.

The coldness in his voice told Abby he'd caught on. Whether he had been involved though, she had yet to discover.

"I've been snowed under, but I can't tell you how happy I am to hear you're looking out for Abby and those boys."

"You can cut the crap, Elizabeth. I know." Abby glanced at her husband attempting to read his expression in the faint light from her mobile screen, adding, "We both know. Everything you told us was a pack of lies."

"Not everything, Abby."

"There never was a car tailing you that night was there?"

Silence. Then, "No. I saw a Lexus from the window and the idea came to me like a flash."

"You have no knowledge of a Dr Fatima Maloof."

"No," Elizabeth repeated, her tone turning wistful. "How can I make you understand?"

"Try talking."

"Very well. Most of what I told you is the truth. Cathy disappeared when she was eighteen. She ran off with a teacher from her high school. Her family were furious with her. She never forgave them for not accepting her marriage to a man fifteen years older than herself." There was a pause before Elizabeth continued in a voice thick with emotion.

"Then it happened exactly as I told you. First her husband's death and then her own, culminating in the boys being shunted from foster home to foster home. Those boys had a happy life. Losing both their parents, seeing their mother die such a painful and slow death, then having to enter the social services system were terrible events for them to deal with alone."

"The note Cathy left, what did that really say? There was no danger was there? No one threatening their lives?"

"You're right, Abby. But I'm not sorry I told those white lies."

"White lies? And what about Roman? Did you really tell him I was in danger? Or did you dream up this plot together?"

Roman reeled back on his feet. "You seriously believe I was involved? Abby!"

Abby met his outranged stare and then shook her head. "No, not really. But you do understand I have to check?"

Tight lipped, he nodded.

Abby exhaled loudly before saying to Elizabeth, "You led Roman to believe I was in danger. He dropped his life in Manila to come here for no good reason. For the past few weeks, I've been bailing up strangers, investigating any new people in town, walking on eggshells each time I heard a noise outside the house at night. We've been dogging those kids' like shadows, checking on them as often as we could." Abby's voice rose.

"I won't apologise, Abby. Because Roman is there with you, with those two homeless boys who so desperately need a loving family. That's what Cathy wanted for them. That's what I wanted for both of you. It's not what or how you thought your family would be, but this is what you all need."

Looking stunned, Roman dragged in a breath as he rubbed a hand over his forehead. "I can't believe I'm hearing this. You made it up?"

"Yes."

The simple word hung in the air like a hand grenade with the pin removed.

Roman shook his head, looking at Abby. "I don't know what to think."

Even though she'd suspected the truth, Abby still had trouble processing the enormity of what her friend had done. She found her voice. "You had no right."

"True. And if you decide to make a complaint about me, which is your right, my career is over. But I'll retire gracefully if only I can be reassured the boys and both of you will have a happy home."

Abby closed her eyes, shaking as a wave of emotions washed over her; anger, betrayal, disbelief … yearning. "It's not what I want," she whispered.

"I know, sweetie," Elizabeth said sadly. "We don't always get what we want but sometimes, sometimes we get something different. Something that can be just as good. Please think about it. Please don't allow your anger with my interference taint your decision. Give this different life a chance."

"I guess we owe the boys that much." Roman touched Abby's cheek with his fingertips but she turned away, lips trembling. "At least there are no more secrets. Unless there is more you haven't told us, Elizabeth?"

"No, I swear." She paused a few seconds then added, "The executor of Cathy's will, has finally released her few possessions to me, together with the log-on details to a cloud server. I have photos of the boys growing up. Of their parents and of all of them together. Cathy was prepared. She'd scanned all her pictures, school awards and exam results, letters she wrote to be given to them, and saved everything on the server. I can forward that information to you, if you like?"

After glancing at Abby's averted face, Roman said, "Yes. We'll make sure the boys receive access, and print out a few photos and get them framed."

"I'll say goodbye then. Please take your time before you decide one way or the other." Elizabeth rang off.

The silence thickened and Abby felt as if all the oxygen in the world had been sucked into a vacuum.

"Abby ..."

"Don't. Not now, Roman. I need to think." Abby stared down at her blank screen.

"Nothing's really changed, though. The boys need a real home, I'm thinking of moving back to Australia ..." His voice trailed off suggestively.

Abby's hand clenched around her phone and she stared at him through the gloomy shadows. "God, Roman! What are you saying? That we make this arrangement permanent? That you move in and we take up our lives as if you'd never left?"

She refused to acknowledge that that scenario had dogged her every waking thought for days.

He compressed his lips, obviously forcing back his own angry response.

She poked his chest. "You turned your back on me.

You said, 'no more'. You wanted your career more than trying another adoption application."

"That's not what happened," he snapped. "Not all of it. I couldn't reach you Abby. You'd turned into someone I didn't recognise. All you cared about, all you seemed to talk about, was having a baby. You breathed it, lived it, every single second of every day. It was as if I didn't exist. You wouldn't listen when the agency suggested counselling."

She sucked in a harsh breath. "So, it's my fault?"

"Shit." He paced in a tight circle. "I didn't say that."

"No, but that's what you implied."

"We were both at fault. We both needed distance."

"Well, that's something we both got, me in Australia and you in the Philippines."

"I would have come back the moment you asked," he ground out. "But you never did, Abby. You never once contacted me."

She enunciated slowly, "You. Left."

"The earthquake …"

"I understood you had a job to do, one that you loved. But you didn't come back to me. You never called again after leaving that message. You blamed me."

He shook his finger and said just as forcefully, "You blamed me."

And there it was, all that anger, disappointment, resentment they'd secretly held against each other, no longer hiding, stark and naked for both of them to see. They'd blamed each other.

Maybe they still blamed each other.

Whirling away from him, Abby rammed her fist into her mouth. Eyes shut, she concentrated on her breathing, on forcing down the pain that screamed to be heard until finally, she gave a heavy sigh. "Nothing's changed."

"Those boys need us."

"No. They need a loving family. This isn't that."

"Rubbish. You know I love you. I know you love me."

"It's not enough! Can't you see? We're broken."

"We're only broken because you can't accept there'll never be a baby for us."

No baby for us.

His words shredded her heart.

That old longing rose up until it damn well near choked her.

No baby.

She swallowed.

Curled her fingers until her nails dug into her palms.

Tried to push the past back where it should remain.

No baby.

But the yearning refused to die.

"Then that's it. There's nothing more to say." She fixed her stare on his pale face. "You need to leave."

Alone, she marched back to the house.

CHAPTER 25

Hands jammed in his overcoat pockets, Roman stood outside the school grounds waiting for the final bell to peel signalling the end to the school day. He'd texted Abby to say he'd pick the boys up and take them to soccer training before dropping them home. He'd also said, *'Don't worry. I won't hang around'.*

Her response was a brief *'Thanks'.*

Their marriage was over.

Disappointment and hurt ate away at his gut like corrosive acid.

How had it come to this?

And why the hell had he allowed himself to hope? Now, there was nothing before him. His burgeoning dream of beginning again with Abby and the challenges of living with two wary teenagers had been ground into dust.

Maybe it *had* been too much to ask of his wife, to think that she could move on. He'd known right from the moment they'd met that her dream was to have a baby of her own.

On their very first date at a café in Bondi, she hadn't held back on letting him know what she wanted from life.

And, God help him, he would have given her the moon on a plate if he could, he loved her so much. He'd been twenty-three, she twenty. They'd believed life was a smorgasbord spread before their feet.

But he hadn't been able to fulfil his promise.

He couldn't give her a child of their own.

Only that morning, he'd booked a one-way ticket to the Philippines. Come Friday, he'd be watching Sydney disappear into the distance from the plane window.

Abby said she wanted him gone.

Well, bloody hell he was going, even though the thought of leaving so soon cramped his gut. He wanted more time.

More time with Abby.

More time with Drew and Eddie.

But he knew you didn't always get what you want.

A gust of chilly wind blew a crumpled paper wrapper across the tarmac, bringing with it the sound of drills and a cutting saw from where tradesmen were hard at work on the new school building to house the kids from years seven to ten. Dust and grit filled his mouth.

He eyed the sky where the clouds were a dark, ominous grey. The regions to the north and east of Bindarra were being thoroughly soaked by two low-pressure systems. The last report on the radio had advised a month's worth of rain had been dumped already in the past seven hours. At least the storm systems were not near

Bindarra but that was no comfort for the towns in their path.

What a crap day.

A couple of cars pulled into the school parking grounds, and parents emerged to huddle in a group for a chat while they waited. One waved to him. He recognised Bridgett, the young French woman he'd met when he'd dropped in to see a local architect, Mark Bradford, when checking the storm damage to his building. She had a young baby snuggled up in a warm, powder-blue onesie cuddled in her arms.

Feeling unable to make friendly conversation, Roman gave a brief smile and walked a few metres away. No one followed.

The bell rang.

Instantly the air was filled with shouting, laughing children of all ages, and the pounding of feet as the kids rushed from their classrooms. They swarmed into the playground, bags bobbing up and down on their backs as they jostled their way to the bus stop or the carpark. Several kids mounted pushbikes and pelted down the road.

A teacher yawned as she crossed the yard to stand amongst the small group of kids waiting for the bus.

The wind had picked up. Grateful for the warmth of his coat, Roman stamped his feet as he scanned the crowd.

Where are they?

The mob of kids was thinning as they dispersed in every direction of the compass. A few kids ran past, greeting their parents, then he heard the sound of car doors slamming, engines starting.

Frowning, Roman looked around the nearly deserted

parking area. Apart from a couple of cars he assumed belonged to teachers, he was alone.

He pulled out his mobile and dialled first Drew and when the call went to voice-mail, he tried Eddie's phone.

Same response.

The school bus trundled down the road and pulled up with the rattling grate of brakes. The waiting kids piled on.

As he watched, the bus pulled out onto the road and set off at a cautious speed.

The teacher turned around and must have spotted him. She began to walk over. Her fair hair was bundled under a beanie and she looked in her early twenties, possibly fresh from teacher's college.

"Hi. Can I help you?"

Roman examined the empty playground then walked to meet her half-way, holding out his hand. "I'm Roman Taylor. Here to pick up Drew and Eddie Kirby. They're new. Only been here a couple of weeks; I'm not certain you know them?"

"I'm Chelsea Morgan, the infants' teacher." She shook his hand and then frowned.

"How do you know them again?"

Deciding it would be easier bending the truth to save time, Roman said, "Abby and I are their foster parents."

"Sorry, I need to make sure you've got the legal right to be here." Chelsea smiled. "Their names aren't ringing any bells, though."

"Red-haired, brown eyes."

"Hmmm, not sure. Come on. They can't be far. We'll look in the classrooms together." Smiling, she beckoned for Roman to follow. "Craig should still be here. He teaches years five and six."

Roman nodded. "He'll be Eddie's teacher then."

They reached the school block.

Chelsea led the way into a classroom a bit farther along the wide verandah. A young man looked up from the papers he was reading as they entered. "Craig, glad you're still here. Roman here is looking for Eddie …" She hesitated.

"Eddie Kirby. A red-haired lad. He should be in your class."

"Of course. I know Eddie. He's a bright student and has gained some confidence since he first arrived." Craig rose and held out his hand. "Craig Sanders." A faint flush appeared on his face as he glanced at the other teacher. "Is there a problem?"

Roman frowned as he looked around the vacant classroom. "I'm here to pick up him and his older brother, Drew."

"Eddie left the classroom with the other kids. You could have missed them."

"No. I arrived well before the final bell rang. I just tried their mobiles, but didn't get an answer."

Craig looked from Roman to Chelsea then back to Roman. An anxious crease appeared in his forehead. "Come to think of it, Eddie was a lot quieter than usual. Is there something going on at home?"

"Why do you say that?" Roman said sharply. Dread was beginning to claw at the pit of his gut.

The younger man's flush deepened. "The principal gave me a brief on Eddie's circumstances. Plus, it's the usual question we ask when kids act differently to their norm. As I said, Eddie wasn't his usual chatterbox self today."

Lips thinned, Roman said, "If you don't mind, I want to do a search of the grounds and every classroom."

"A good idea. I'll come with you." Craig hurried back to his desk where he grabbed his mobile.

"And I'll get the principal." Chelsea left the room.

Twenty minutes later, Roman was satisfied neither boy was anywhere in or around the school. Craig offered to contact the parents of their friends and while he was obtaining their numbers from the principal's office, Roman walked off to the carpark where he phoned the boys' mobiles again.

And again, no one picked up.

He left messages for them to call him back straight away.

Standing there, with the rising wind buffeting his body, Roman clenched his fists.

This shouldn't be happening.

He thought back to last night when he and Abby had had their bitter fight near the chicken coop. There'd been a moment when he'd imagined a footstep. At the time, he'd dismissed the notion after checking for any movement. Now he wasn't so sure. If one of the boys, likely Drew, the kid was more suspicious than his brother, had overhead Abby say they were about to be sent back …

Shit.

He whirled around as footsteps hurried towards him. The two young teachers, concern etched in their pale faces.

Craig panted out, "No one has seen them since school ended."

"Thanks for your help. I need to phone my wife." Roman slid inside his rental car and rang Abby.

She picked up straight away.

"Abby, are the boys with you?"

"No. I haven't seen them since this morning." A pause. "Aren't they at the school?" Her voice turned abrupt.

"No. They left before I arrived. I've tried both their mobile numbers and got nothing. I also asked the teacher to phone their friends' parents, but they haven't seen them."

"Maybe they decided to walk with one of their mates to a shop or something."

A little of his tension eased. Roman said, "That's possible. Sorry. I could be stressing over nothing. Only that …"

"What? What is it, Roman?"

He said slowly, "I did wonder whether Drew overheard us arguing."

"Damn." Abby inhaled sharply. "Maybe you could cruise around town? I'll phone Hester, Marsha and Natalie and ask them to contact their kids. They could be playing footy."

"Good idea. I'll check the footy field first." Roman started his car. "Abby, as soon as I spot them, I'll phone you."

"Thanks. And I'll let you know how I get on with their friends' parents. Don't worry. We'll find them." She rang off.

Abby was right. He was probably over-reacting. But his gut had never let him down in the past.

Frowning, Roman pulled out onto the road and began his search.

CHAPTER 26

Sunset came and went and by ten o'clock, an official search was underway. Roman continually checked the police Facebook page where an amber alert had been issued. A sighting of the boys near the Caltex service station located on the other side of Kingfisher Bridge had sent him and Abby racing to the area. But it was either a false alarm or the boys were long gone.

As the night marched on, the chances of finding them before morning dwindled.

They decided to split up, Abby returning to the search with her police colleagues and Roman going alone.

He drummed his fingers on the steering wheel as he drove slowly along Kings Road in the hope the boys had kept walking in that direction. They could be attempting to hitch a lift out of town. Heading for the border. Heading for the coast.

Hell. They could have been anywhere.

All Roman knew for certain was they weren't heading home.

That's because they don't have one.

Not a real one. Not a home with parents who love them.

All they had was the knowledge they were off to another foster home and who knew how many other foster homes after that?

The savage thought slammed into his mind. For the first time, he wondered whether he could go it alone, apply to foster them as a single parent. It was a far cry from growing old with the woman he loved, but during the past couple of weeks, those two boys had taken a big hold on his heart. It was obvious they loved the country life, another reason for them not to leave.

We could move to another small town, me and the boys.
Start afresh and build a life together.

It would be hard as he saw the hope in Drew and Eddie's eyes each time they looked at Abby. But staying in Bindarra Creek and not being with her would be too painful for everyone concerned.

Money wasn't a problem. He wasn't a millionaire, but he'd been paid well over the years in his risky career, and everyone knew houses were cheaper in country areas. They would do okay.

His mobile rang. It was Abby.

His pulse thundered in his ears as he clicked the Bluetooth connection. "Hey, hon. Any sign of them?"

"No. What about you?" Her voice sounded strained, close to breaking point.

Easing off the accelerator, Roman squeezed his eyes shut for a second. Upon opening them he took another long look out the window. Nothing to see but dark paddocks and fields. The boys could be hiding beneath a tree or bush and he could have driven straight past them. "Nothing, but it's too dark to see very far."

"Oh, God, Roman. It's getting so late. Where can they be?"

"We'll find them, Abby. Hang in there, hon," he said fiercely.

She was silent for a few moments before she whispered, "What if we don't?"

"I don't believe anyone has taken them. The logical explanation is they overheard us last night and have run away. They could have felt rejected," he said, deliberately keeping his voice calm. Like he was in control. Like he wasn't falling apart inside.

"I've been such a fool." She hiccupped as if she'd been crying.

He'd sensed she was more emotionally involved than she'd admit. But how much, was the question. Did she care enough to let go of the past?

He didn't know and now wasn't the time for soul searching.

Not when two homeless boys were missing.

"We'll keep looking, Abby. We won't stop. They can't have gotten far. They haven't a lot of money."

"I raced home and checked. I had fifty dollars stashed in a jar behind the coffee pot. It's gone."

"Still not enough to get them a great distance," he reassured her.

"True. I'm panicking, Roman. I'm not dealing with this very well. I keep calling their phones but they're not answering."

Same, he thought. "Think like a cop, Abby. You're the best police officer I know."

A long, drawn-out sigh came over the speaker. "You're right, Roman. It's time I put aside my emotions and work this case properly."

"That's my girl."

Her choked-off sob wrenched at his own heartstrings. He felt the burn of tears scour his eyes and scrubbed them away with the back of his hand.

"Right, then. I'm going to park the wagon and walk down every street in town. I'll look behind every building and knock on every door. We will find them." Her firm tone eased a little of the anxiety he held for her emotional state.

"Want me to turn back? I'm about thirty K's out of town on Kings Road."

"Maybe keep going until you reach a hundred? If they're still missing when you get back, you can join me on the foot search. AJ is working on contacting their mobile phone providers for their recent history, and Sarge is interviewing their friends."

"I thought I'd get the SES involved. I'm worried about the river rising. Warren spoke about his concerns on the river levels at the first SES meeting I went to."

"Yes. Damn. That's something I hadn't considered."

"I've contacted Warren and asked him to reach out to other SES stations where their towns are close to either the Akuna River or Bindarra Creek. Get us an update on the levels in their areas."

"Good thinking, Roman. A flood is the last thing we need," Abby sighed. "But there's no rain forecast for us."

"Doesn't have to be, given Bindarra is situated in a valley, and with the rivers feeding from areas where rain is falling," he said. "Dodge has a couple of teams on standby. Do you think we should rope them in on the foot search?"

"Let's give it another couple of hours. If there's no change, definitely phone him. But they'll need to co-ordinate the search with us."

"I'm on it, babe."

A weighted silence strung between them before Abby spoke again. "Roman, thank you."

"I'm where I'm meant to be, Abby, with you."

When she didn't respond, he ended the call.

The long hours ticked by as the night grew steadily colder. Roman arrived back in town a little after eleven thirty and immediately phoned Abby. He came across her poking about the skip bins behind the bowling club and about to do another walk through Lette Park.

"I'm here," he called.

She looked up.

Their eyes met.

With a sob, she ran towards him.

She collapsed onto his chest and all but strangled him with her arms as she clung to his shoulders.

He held on just as tight, his face buried in her soft hair that had escaped its clasp.

"I'm here, babe."

"They haven't come home."

"I know. I know. We'll find them."

She leaned back, and peered at him through the gloom. "But it's so cold."

"They've got jackets, beanies and gloves. They'll be fine. All we have to do is find them."

Releasing her hold, she stepped back then wiped her

nose. "The SES are out in full, as are Riley and AJ. That is so wonderful of them."

Roman nodded. "But only until two thirty. Riley's going to call the search off then until morning."

"I'm not stopping." Her eyes snapped, fierce with steely resolve.

Reaching out, he took hold of her cold hands. "Neither am I."

CHAPTER 27

At around four in the morning, Roman insisted they stop and take a break. They trudged back to the police station where a tired AJ still manned the radio. The instant Abby sat down, her eyes closed. Exhaustion claimed her, dragging her under into a troubled sleep.

She was struggling in a dream where she chased Drew and Eddie along the track in the Akuna National Park. She ran and ran and ran, never catching them. And the more she ran, the farther away they seemed to get. Then Roman appeared out of the bushes, his hands spread wide, distress in his eyes. *'Where's the baby?',* he begged.

'There is no baby', she wailed.

He touched her shoulder. *'Where's the boys?'*

The boys! Panic strangled at her throat, choking her as she looked and looked and looked. The track vanished into a thick grey fog that stretched in every direction. Around and around she spun, but Drew and Eddie were nowhere to be seen.

"Abby! Come on, hon. Wake up!" Roman's beseeching

voice and the feel of his hands on her shoulders, pulled her from the nightmare.

"What?" Pushing hair from her eyes, she sat up, feeling groggy and sick to her stomach.

Her desperate gaze moved past him.

Drew! Eddie!

They weren't there.

"The boys?"

"No sign of them yet." Eyes a stormy grey, he studied her face and gave a tight smile. "That was some dream you were having. I thought you were going to roll right off the bunk."

"Yeah, it was horrible." She placed her hands over her face for a moment. Removing them, she looked around and frowned. "Where am I?"

This smile was more genuine. "In a cell. I carried you here so you could kip out for a few hours."

"Oh no! What's the time?" She staggered to her feet, the police-issue blanket tangling around her legs.

"Here, let me help." He tossed the blanket aside and cupped a hand under her elbow. "It's six in the morning. Still no sign of them. The last and only sighting was at the service station."

"They can't have vanished into thin air." Abby shuddered, as she remembered how the boys had disappeared in her dream.

"I agree. They're close. I know it." He soothed her mussed hair away from her face and pressed a soft kiss to her mouth. "We need to talk about this, hon."

"I know we do, but I can't, not now, not until we find them." She managed a smile. "I'm so glad you're here with me."

"I wouldn't be anywhere else." He soothed his fingers over her forehead, giving her temples a slight massage.

Pulling away, she muttered, "I need a shower and a toothbrush. We need to get back out there."

"Abby, wait," Roman said as she began to head for the staff amenities.

Whirling around, she stopped. Her belly clenched as she noticed the fatigue shadowing his face.

"There's something you have to know."

Breath shuddering, she pressed a hand to her chest where her heart gave a painful jolt. "What is it?"

"The SES have issued a warning. The river is rising, and there's a shit-load of water heading our way. It's possible Bindarra will be hit with a flash flood sometime today."

※

THE SEARCH HAD CONTINUED all morning and after her dream, Abby insisted she and Roman check out the national park but with no luck. The sight of the heavily swollen river surging through the gorge had done little to ease their worry. Now they were back in town, and keen to re-join the search there. Half the SES members had splintered off to begin flood mitigation control and warn the residents living in the low-lying areas along the creek and Akuna River.

Sweaty despite the cold day, and feeling like her eyes had been rubbed raw with sandpaper, Abby entered the CWA hall and accepted the proffered tea with a nod of thanks. She was so tired she could hardly talk, but Edwina seemed to understand.

The old lady patted her shoulder and whispered, "It will be all right. Have faith, my dear." Then she bustled off to where a group of CWA ladies were handing out sandwiches and hot drinks whenever a search member staggered inside, desperate for refreshment.

"The town's behind us, Abby." Roman slung an arm over her shoulders. "The Beasleys and Wangs have joined the search. And Natalie and her son are re-checking the kids' favourite hang-outs."

Abby sagged against the wall. and gulped her sweet, milky tea, anxious to finish and begin again.

"Steady on." Roman pressed half a ham sandwich into her hand. "Eat it." He devoured his half in three seconds.

"Want another?" Smiling wanly, she offered hers.

"No. I'm hungry but I feel if I eat any more, I'll puke all over the place."

"Me too." Sighing, she forced the food down then dusted the crumbs from her fingers.

Roman drained the last of his tea and tossed both their styrene cups into a garbage bin. He straightened, pulling her up with him. Capturing her chin with his fingers, he murmured, his voice deep with tightly-held emotion, "Whatever happens, we're in this together. I'm not leaving this time."

Nodding, Abby scrubbed at her eyes. Words were beyond her.

And besides, she had no idea how she would answer even if she could.

Hand-in-hand, they left the hall, and after climbing into the paddy wagon, they drove to the SES station which was where the search was being co-ordinated from.

The station was a hive of activity.

Warren Myers used a megaphone to shout instructions to a bunch of volunteers who were sandbagging in the carpark. As Abby and Roman drove past the gates, two utes roared out. She recognised Grady and Opal in one, the rear tray crammed with yellow roadblock barriers. The other car, carrying similar gear, held Dodge and Sara. They waved before disappearing down the road.

"They're going to barricade all the bridges leading in and out of town. Plus, a couple of causeways. We don't want anyone attempting to cross while the river is so high," Roman told her.

Abby frowned. "I hope no one does anything stupid." She parked the wagon and together, they walked into the station.

Senior Sergeant Riley Morgan, AJ, Leslie Wolski and the Westburys were gathered around a map spread over a large desk at the front of the hall.

Looking up, Riley made eye contact, and waved them over. "We've got a watch-and-act advice out for the river and a lot of members are still door knocking. They're not only issuing the river warning but also asking about the boys."

"Thanks," Abby muttered. She shifted her weight from foot to foot, wondering what was bugging her. Something she'd seen? Something she'd heard? Someone?

"We're expecting people to begin arriving soon for sandbags." Riley walked over to the wall where a map of Bindarra Creek hung. He pointed out various streets, mainly to the southwest of town. "The BC Retirement Home backs onto fields running beside the river. There are a few villas on the outer edges of the block which are low-lying. AJ and I will take a drive out there now and assist the manager and staff evacuating any affected residents. We've asked the manager of the caravan park to organise moving the vans closest to the river."

Thoughtful, Abby walked closer.

Strange how you could live in a town but still be oblivious to things like flood-prone areas. Her gaze settled on the cemetery and the church as she recalled the events of last week. It made her think of the brief glimpse she'd had of Sara sitting beside Dodge, heading out to work together. She'd only seen her for a second or two, but the woman had radiated an aura of tranquillity so different to the sullen, depressed creature they'd found near the caravan park.

The caravan park.

Riley had mentioned the caravan park.

Eagerly Abby turned to Roman, gripping his shirt in both hands. "The caravan park. It's got vacant vans, hasn't it?"

Roman looked over at Riley. "Has anyone checked the park?"

"AJ? You've got the list." Riley nodded at Constable Donaldson.

Flushing, AJ croaked, "It was checked last night and given the all-clear."

"In the dark, it would be easy to miss a broken lock or window," Roman pointed out. His hands covered hers. "It's worth another look."

She nodded, then switched her gaze to her senior sergeant.

Riley nodded. "Go. Check with the manager while

you're there. I can't raise him on his mobile, and I want a status update on getting those vans out of harm's way."

"No worries, Sarge."

Abby burned rubber getting to the park in record time and jumped out of the wagon the instant she killed the engine, saying, "This is it, Roman. They have to be here."

Equally fired up, Roman came around the front of the wagon in a rush. "I believe they'll be in a van situated well away from the others. Drew's smart. He'd know to keep a low profile."

"Agreed." Abby examined the park for a second. "Let's start with the last row and work our way inward."

They jogged down the narrow, tarred road that wound through the park, passing the manager who was using a tractor to tow a van out of the danger zone. Several residents trudged past, hauling bags and boxes of possessions. A few led dogs on leads. One bright spark pushed a wheelbarrow piled high with bulging garbage bags on which perched his Persian cat. A ute trundled after them, the tray crammed with furniture and odds and sods.

"Good to see they've heeded the warning. This entire park slopes towards the river," Roman muttered. "I bet a good third could lie in the hundred-year flood zone."

They reached the boundary where a stretch of stubby grass-covered ground fell steeply to the riverbank. Several lots were vacant, obviously set aside for tourists, and Abby and Roman made their way along the row, checking each van together.

But they were all empty.

"They're not here." Panic, anguish, and worry rose like a maelstrom from her belly. Abby bent over, retching up her meagre lunch.

Murmuring soothing noises, Roman rubbed her back until the tempest passed.

Her radio crackled.

Wiping her mouth, she pulled it from her duty belt and rasped, "Abby here, over."

"Abby! Roman! Get away from there!" ordered Riley.

"Sarge? What …?"

"You've got a wall of water three metres high coming your way. Get out! *Now!*"

Roman was already moving, tugging her along and forcing her into a run as they raced through the park. They reached the residents.

"Run!" yelled Roman, ushering them forward.

Screaming and crying, the crowd raced for higher ground.

Abby heard it.

A furious roar that filled her ears and head with white noise.

There was a massive bang.

Another crack, like the boom of a cannon, rent the air.

"What was that?" she screamed, as she lurched to a halt.

Face taut, Roman shook his head, and tugged her forward again.

The mind-numbing rush of sound was almost upon them.

She scooped up an elderly pooch struggling on his stiffly rheumatic legs, while Roman hoisted his equally elderly owner into his arms.

"Go! Go!" shouted Roman, to the crowd.

Stumbling and scrambling, everyone fled up the slope.

They came to a staggering halt near the amenities

block. The manager ran towards them, waving his hands madly in the air, "What's happening?"

"Flash flood!" Abby called back

Huddling close to Roman, she shut her eyes as the crescendo of noise filled her ears.

Gradually, the roar diminished to a steady torrent.

Were they safe?

Holding her breath, Abby craned her neck to gaze towards the river.

"I think the danger's passed. I'm going back to check the river levels." Roman placed the old lady on the ground.

Abby handed over the dog. "I'll come with."

They ran down the sloping road but before they came to the edge of the park, they saw the full impact of the devastation. The river was frothing a metre from the boundary fence, like a writhing, furious snake.

"Look! The Gillies Bridge has collapse!" Abby pointed.

"I think ..." Roman grabbed her arm, spinning her around to face downstream. "Isn't that Sara's car?"

Abby watched the Volkswagen pitch from side to side as it floated near the edge of the river. Her mobile rang.

Drew shrieked, "Abby! Abby! We're trapped!"

Before the car disappeared from view, a small hand thrust out of the side window.

CHAPTER 28

For three seconds, Abby couldn't breathe. Couldn't think. Couldn't move.

Drew.

Eddie.

Roman yanked her radio from her duty belt and began barking instructions to AJ while calling the SES station with his mobile in his other hand. After speaking, he turned to Abby. "The closest team is seven minutes away. We don't have that much time. Come on!"

"We've got no equipment." Abby stayed him by grabbing his arm.

"Every minute counts."

Her breath clawed at her throat at his grim expression. "I know. Maybe someone has a life jacket? I saw a kayak beside one of the vans."

Roman took one last look at the river then nodded, his fingers reaching and finding hers.

Turning around, Abby was about to break into a run only to find the park residents gathered behind them.

"Oh, my lord. Is someone stuck in that car?" A woman pressed her hand to her mouth.

"Yes." Abby choked out. "Our ... our boys."

The manager stepped forward. "How can we help?"

Roman said, "Paddles, rope, lots of rope, any life jackets?"

The manager whirled around, shouting, "You heard the man! Move, people!"

Several residents took off.

"And the tractor," Roman added. "Just in case."

Understanding flashed over the manager's face. "Okay. Okay. I'll move the tractor further along the river." He raced away, calling for a couple of blokes to give him a hand unhooking the van.

Looking at Abby, Roman said, "If we can secure a rope to the car, maybe we can tow it to shore."

"And if we can't?"

"I'll swim."

"Roman." Abby cupped his face in her hands.

"No time, babe."

She nodded. Taking back her radio, she gave AJ a quick update, talking while they ran down the slope towards the river.

They jumped over the fence and raced along the edge of swiftly moving water. Roman threw off his bulky coat and woolly jumper as they ran.

"There! I see it!" Abby pointed to where the tail end of the car peeped out from the branches of a tree. The river surge had swallowed the bank and risen high, swirling around the trunk of a small tree with low-growing branches.

She craned her neck. "Thank heavens, the tree has

stopped the car from being swept out farther. It appears to be wedged against a branch."

"I'll climb out on the limb and with luck, we can get them out that way." Roman turned around. "Where's that rope?"

"Here you go, mate." A heavily tattooed fellow with a grey beard handed over three coils of rope and his motorbike helmet.

Another bloke arrived, panting, two life jackets in one hand and a paddle in the other. Three other men and two women followed.

"Right, this is what we're going to do." Roman popped the helmet onto his head and did up the straps.

"Who's a champion thrower?"

"I am." One of the women stepped forward.

"Me," said one of the men.

"We need a back-up plan in case the branch doesn't hold, and the kids get swept down the river. You two are on the ropes. Wade out but not too far. Be careful. The river is still packing a lot of power. Watch for my signal. When I wave my hands in the air, throw the ropes out at this angle." Roman crouched, and quickly assembled a diagram on the ground using twigs and stones.

"If they fall into the river, you haul them back in. You and you help steady the person with the rope, and pull as well, if you have to. Don't panic. Keep hauling the boys to shore. Got it?"

Everyone nodded.

"Take my torch. It's waterproof." Abby clipped her torch off her belt.

"Wait here." Roman pinned her with a stern look until she nodded.

He stood, shoved the life jackets down his shirt then ran the shortest rope around his chest, securing it tight. After clamping the torch between his teeth, he waded into the river.

Abby was horrified to see the river had risen so high, the water now lapped around his waist. A few seconds later, Roman climbed onto the branch.

Heart in her mouth, Abby watched as he forced his way through the thick foliage.

The car dropped lower in the water.

"It's sinking." She moved closer, uncaring of the water sloshing over her boots.

She could see one of the boys close to the window, hammering on the glass. Then she spotted Roman. He had his legs wrapped around the branch and was leaning over the car. He rapped the window, and one of the boys wound it down. He worked loose the rope holding the life jackets in place and shoved them inside.

The tree creaked.

"Oh my God! Oh my God! The car's moving!" someone screamed.

They were right. The surge was slowly turning the car, forcing the backend to swing out into deeper water. Any second and the car could be swept away.

The two people holding the ropes exchanged glances, then waded into the water. Their support people close behind.

The wail of sirens rapidly approaching, filled the air. The firies, the police. But would they be in time to help Roman?

They needed more time, but time, wasn't on their side.

Abby snapped off her duty belt. Fingers shaking, she

removed the bullets from her gun, shoving them into her pocket before rushing back to the watching crowd. She gave the belt and gun to a woman, telling her to hand it over to the police when they arrived.

She rushed into the water until the river swirled around her knees.

Body tense, braced to dive in the second she had to, Abby waited, holding her breath as Roman banged on the car's bonnet.

The bloody thing jolted.

Shifted.

Turned faster.

Someone tapped her shoulder, and looking behind, she saw the tractor lumbering into view, the manager white-faced but determined. After one horrified glance at the scene, he accelerated and sent the tractor bumping along the river's edge, obviously hoping to get in front of the car.

"He's got him!" A woman pointed.

Abby spun back to see Roman hauling Eddie out of the car. First his arms, head and torso and finally his legs. Roman pulled the boy up onto the branch but the weight was too much.

Crack!

The branch split in two. In a flail of legs and arms, Roman and Eddie tumbled into the water with an almighty splash.

Freed from its restraints, the Volkswagen lurched as the current took hold.

"Oh my God! It's moving farther out," croaked Abby, her frantic gaze swinging between the car and the spot where she'd last seen her husband.

Then Roman bobbed to the surface, one arm thrust into the air, his other arm supporting Eddie.

"Now!" screamed Abby.

The woman threw her rope.

It splashed into the river,

The current sent the rope weaving and twisting towards where Roman struggled to keep Eddie's head above water as the river ploughed around them in a froth of leaves, branches and heaving waves.

He stretched out, and grabbed the rope. One-handed, he looped it around Eddie's chest. Eddie grabbed hold with both hands. Roman did a thumbs up, and the woman began to pull Eddie to shore.

Fist to her mouth, Abby let out a thankful sob.

Roman turned back to strike out for the car. But the river now had it in its greedy grasp, propelling the car farther downstream.

In the shallows, Abby kept pace. From behind she heard someone yell out that the boy was okay.

Eddie had made it.

Another sob erupted from her chest and Abby stumbled, her foot going down a hole in the mud.

Ahead of her, the Volkswagen pitched back and forth, sinking lower.

Drew was scrambling through the window, struggling to get onto the roof.

Roman swam towards the swiftly moving vehicle. He was almost there.

Drew was half out of the car, clinging to the roof, one leg hooked through the window, the other scrabbling for a foothold on the wet metal.

A massive wave broke over the car, completely submerging it.

Roman dived.

Abby screamed and raced into the river.

Someone tried to haul her back, but she fought them off.

She plunged into the icy water and began to swim. Waves crashed over her head.

Coughing, spluttering, she battled on, not once taking her eyes off the spot where the car had been. A couple of metres from her, a head with red hair plastered to his scalp emerged.

Drew.

His eyes were closed.

Roman popped up beside him, gulping for air, and holding the boy's head out of the water with one arm, he went to raise his other arm.

Another wave broke over their heads, rolling them over.

They went under again.

Abby reached where they'd been a second ago. Holding her breath, she dived beneath the water, fighting against the crazy-fast current. The water was muddy. Impossible to see a thing. Her lungs burned.

Then she spotted the thin beam of her torch.

She struggled closer, each stroke a battle. Something painfully solid whacked her knee. Her hands weaved through the water, frantically searching, groping until a hand gripped hers.

With every atom of strength she possessed, she struck for the sun shining in the sky above, hauling her beloveds with her.

Lungs straining, she emerged, gasping and choking as Roman and Drew surfaced beside her.

Roman spewed a gutful of water back into the river.

Coughing and spluttering, as the river dragged them farther downstream, Abby waved her arm in the air.

A rope slapped into the water. It swept towards them.

She swam for it, grabbed a section.

Roman slammed into her side and they plummeted below the surface again in a tumble of limbs.

But the rope tightened and began to move.

She held on. Up she bobbed, gasping for air, as she slid through the water. She risked a glance over her shoulder.

Roman was right behind her, the end of the rope wrapped several times around his wrist and dragging Drew, dear Drew, with them.

Finally, her feet found the clinging mud bottom.

Eager hands reached out and pulled them from the river.

Chest heaving, Abby collapsed onto the sand, her gaze seeking and finding Roman cradling Drew in his arms.

Roman met her anxious eyes. "He's okay. Knocked his head against the side of the car."

Drew groaned and began to stir.

Roman advised him to remain still until the ambos arrived, then rubbed a hand over his pale face. Blood seeped from a cut above his eyes.

"Abby! Roman! Where's Drew?" Eddie pushed through the gathering crowd. Some kind person had thrown a blanket around him. He hobbled towards her then flung himself into Abby's lap, sobbing.

As she stroked his hair with a trembling hand, she

soothed, "Hey, it's okay. Drew's okay. We're all safe. It's over."

Over his bent head, her tear-filled eyes met her husband's and she said, "Thank you."

They'd all been given a second chance at life.

Now, all they had to do was live it.

CHAPTER 29

When they arrived at the hospital, the waiting room of the ER was packed with injured people. But the moment they staggered inside on the arms of the paramedics, a triage nurse pushed through the throng.

"Shawn. Good to see you again," Abby said to the brawny male nurse.

He grimaced as he indicated the pile of people waiting for attention. "I'd prefer we'd met at the pub over a pint. Now, what have we got here?"

After a quick assessment, Shawn waved them through the double doors where they were soon seen by the doctor. After a few minutes prodding and peering at Roman's forehead, Dr Frobisher declared his wound didn't require stitches. He was passed off onto the nurse for her to dress it while the doctor checked the boys over.

"They've going to be very sore tomorrow from bruising, and Eddie's right wrist is definitely sprained. I'll get Shawn to bind it and give him a script for the pain. A week at the most, and he should be right as rain. It's possible Drew has a mild concussion. Bed rest for the next twelve hours." Dr Frobisher gave Abby a brief smile. "Keep an eye on them and bring them back if you have any concerns. Now, what about you?"

Abby straightened, taking care she didn't place her full weight on her left leg. Her knee still throbbed like crazy. "Some scrapes and bruising and my knee took a battering, but I'll live."

The doctor bade her push up her trouser leg and took a few moments to examine her knee. "It's quite swollen. You can adjust your clothes now. If the pain gets worse, or your leg fails to improve, make an appointment with your GP. Now, if you don't mind, I have other patients to attend. Check with the triage nurse on your way out for the script."

"Will do. And thank you, Doctor." Abby turned to the boys.

In the yellow fluorescent lighting, their faces appeared pallid with a sickly tinge. She noted the strained expression in their eyes.

Drew shivered where he stood, water dripping from his wet clothes to puddle on the floor.

Eddie's blue-tinged lips wobbled.

"I'm sorry. This was my fault." Drew looked over at his brother, then squaring his shoulders faced Abby and Roman. "Eddie didn't want to run away, but I convinced him."

Abby said softly, "You heard us arguing."

He nodded.

"Oh, Drew. I'm the one who's sorry." Abby reached out and gave his cold hands a gentle squeeze, smiling at them both. "Now, I need to get you out of those wet clothes before you catch a cold."

"Yeah, I'm freezing." Looking like he wanted to say more but didn't know how, Drew hugged his waist.

"Have you got the scripts?" Abby asked Roman.

He swept a keen gaze over her face before examining the boys. "Yes, and some painkillers. How is everyone?"

"We'll do. The kids need dry clothes."

Roman nodded. "There's a stash of spare clothes at the SES station. I'm sorry, hon, but my phone's been buzzing with messages. I need to get back there."

"I understand. The river is still rising, and you've got a job to do. As do I. We need every able-bodied person helping until the crisis passes." She grimaced. "I don't want to leave the boys alone, though."

Roman forked his hand through his hair. "They can help out at the station, and I'll make certain someone is there if I need to leave. They can take calls, make coffee and write up the incidents on the whiteboard. And there are bunks for them to rest, especially Drew if he feels unwell. I'll keep their minds busy, so they don't start thinking too much about what almost happened."

If anyone knew how to deal with people after a traumatic event, it was Roman. Abby sighed with relief. "Sounds a good idea, but I don't want to leave them."

"I know, hon." He brushed her cheek with his knuckles.

Abby's radio crackled, and she sighed. "Duty calls and other people need our help. I feel better though, knowing they're with you."

"Don't worry. They'll be fine. And I'll be working on my speech where they're grounded for life."

Abby gave a wan chuckle. She wagged her finger at Drew and Eddie. "Do not, under any circumstances, leave the station unless Roman says it's safe to do so. And the second you get there, I want those wet clothes off and dry ones on. And have a quick shower. That will warm you up."

The boys nodded furiously.

Roman added, "I'll get some hot noodle soup into them, too."

"Don't think you're going to wiggle out of this one either. We'll be discussing your punishment for wandering off like this as soon as we're home." Abby turned a stern face towards them, determined to impress, the seriousness of their actions upon them.

Eyes overbright with tears, Eddie burst out, "I won't. Ever!"

"Are you still sending us back?" Shoulders hunched, Drew hugged himself.

The question seemed to punch through the air with the velocity of a bullet.

Abby sucked in a shocked breath while beside her, she felt Roman stiffen as he waited for her answer. She cleared her constricted throat. "I never said that, but I know we've got a lot to talk about. Let's leave this discussion for when we've all had a good sleep."

"What about Pinky? And Geronimo?" Eddie wailed, tears slipping down his cheeks.

"Don't worry, Eddie. Pinky is locked safely inside the house and she has plenty of food and water. And Geronimo has the barn to go to if he feels scared." She hesitated, her heart thudding uncomfortably hard, her hands suddenly shaky.

She didn't want to say goodbye. She wanted to gather them close in her arms. Hold onto them. Never let them go.

Instead, she hooked her thumbs into her duty belt and rocked back on her sodden shoes. "Remember what I said."

Both Drew and Eddie nodded, heads drooping, scuffing their feet.

Roman scrutinised Abby's face for a moment before, placing an arm around the boys' shoulders. "Don't worry. I won't let them out of my sight. Let's go before I turn into a pillar of ice. Bloody hell, I'm cold." He gave a dramatic shiver causing the boys to crack tentative grins.

"Keep in contact with me," Abby tapped her radio.

"Will do." Roman propelled the boys forward and into the waiting room. "Grady Flannigan has messaged he's waiting outside to pick us up."

"I'll radio for AJ to do the same for me." Abby followed them.

Roman paused, swung around then captured Abby's face in his cold hands. The kiss he placed on her lips was fierce, desperate with a longing she could no longer deny.

Abby flung her arms around his neck and pressed tight against him, rejoicing as her soul sang with a desperate hunger until they broke apart.

Roman brushed his thumb over her trembling lips. "Catch you later."

"That's a promise I won't let you break," Abby whispered.

One last smile, and he strode to the door. Then, Eddie came running back to wrap his arms around Abby's waist.

Eyes stinging with tears, she hugged him back. "I'll call you as soon as I can."

Eddie raced back to his brother standing by the door, waiting for him. Drew waved, then they hurried across the tarmac to where a twin-cab ute stood, engine idling. Abby watched as the three of them climbed inside and then the car was gone.

She pressed her knuckles against her eyes before rubbing her hands up and down her cold arms. The hospital's heating was going flat-chat but the chill she felt was too deep to be vanquished by the warmth. She needed a hot shower and dry clothes.

And more coffee.

Blue and red flashing lights swept past as the paddy-wagon drew up.

Abby crossed over to meet AJ as he ushered Pamela Brown inside the hospital. Although wrapped up in a knee-length coat with a knitted scarf around her neck, the elderly lady's teeth visibly chattered.

Abby frowned. "Goodness. What happened?"

"I tink she's okay. Just needs to warm up. I found her in the cemetery." AJ smiled, his face brightening as he looked over Abby's shoulder. "Mum. Dad. I tought you'd be here, helping. Mrs Brown needs a bit of attention."

"We'll see to her, AJ. Come along, Pamela. Barry will settle you in a chair and get you a hot drink." Gloria bustled up, her husband close behind, and laid a gentle hand on Pamela's arm. She lowered her voice, "A blanket too, Barry, if you can find one."

"Leave it to me, love. AJ, be careful out there." The mayor took a moment to grip his son's shoulder.

AJ nodded.

Seemingly satisfied, Barry Donaldson smiled at Abby, then steered the old lady off to a vacant chair.

"My Barry will look after her. He is a good man. Not a clever one, but the kindest man I know." Gloria turned to look at Abby. "He loves this town and everyone in it. He will know how to help Pamela. These past few days have been hard on her. You know what happened?"

Abby shook her head.

Gloria sighed. "Poor lady. You found her in the cemetery, did you say, AJ?"

"Yes, Mum."

"No doubt visiting the graves of her husband and only child. They both drowned, you see, when the Akuna River flooded about thirty-four years ago. Her son was only eighteen."

"How terribly sad." Abby watched the mayor enfold the old lady in a warm blanket. He crouched down beside her chair and taking her hands in his, began to talk.

Gloria followed her glance. "Yes, this weather reminds her of what she lost. We are hoping she will allow Roy to give her happier memories and learn to live for today."

All this time, the poor woman's heart had remained in the past. Abby frowned slightly. Was there a hidden message behind Gloria's words?

"Now, AJ." Gloria eyed her son up and down. "I assume you are still on duty?"

"Yes, Mum," he repeated.

"Then be careful. Now, go. Do your work."

He stooped and kissed her cheek.

Grinning, she shooed him off with her hands.

"We need to stop at the station first, AJ, for me to

change. I've got spare clothes in my locker." About to follow him, Abby paused when Gloria caught her wrist.

"AJ, I need to speak to Abby for a moment." Gloria raised her thin eyebrows at Abby. "You do not mind? It will not be for long."

"Very well." Abby braced herself. The seriousness of the other woman's gaze indicated whatever she intended to say, Abby may not like it.

"I see you with your family here."

"Yes." Abby swallowed hard, then added, "There was an incident at the caravan park where a car was washed downriver by the flash flood."

Gloria gasped. "But that is terrible! I take it no one was seriously hurt? I am glad your family is okay."

For some reason, Abby needed to keep repeating information the other woman already knew, as if by continually reminding people she would accept it herself as truth. "They're not really my family. My husband and I … we're about to divorce. And Eddie and Drew are foster kids I'm looking after for a short time."

But the words tasted bitter on Abby's lips and she could no longer deny the pain in her heart.

The other woman snorted. "After that kiss? I do not think so. Listen, my dear, if you please." She smiled so sweetly Abby found herself unable to move away. "My family was poor. We lived in a squalor it is hard to imagine now. To feed my little brothers and sisters, I became a prostitute."

Uncertain what to say about this revelation, Abby kept quiet.

Gloria shrugged. "I am not proud of what I did, but with no education, what else could I do? Then my Barry found me. He lifted me out of my miserable life and gave me hope of a new one. I was honest. I told him I'd had an abortion when very young. There would be no babies for us. He did not care. He is such a sweet man."

Shaken, Abby touched the older woman's hand. "I'm so sorry, Mrs Donaldson."

"Thank you, my dear." Gloria pulled a tissue from her pocket and wiped her damp eyes. "But I so wanted a child and my Barry wanted me happy."

Gloria gazed earnestly at Abby. "Now we have four wonderful children who complete our lives. We love them with all our hearts. AJ came to us when he was ten from St Lucia in the Caribbean. Our two eldest daughters are Indian and are sisters we adopted when they were eight and twelve. Our youngest, Coralie, is from my home country. Such a sweet girl."

A proud smile chased away the last of her tears. "Delhi, that's our eldest, phoned only yesterday to tell us she is getting married and is expecting a child. So I will get to hold a baby in my arms after all."

"Why are you telling me this?" whispered Abby, her eyes burning.

"I think you know why." Gloria looked over at Pamela. "Leave the past where it belongs, my dear. Open your heart to love. It will find you."

She turned back to Abby and smiled. "Perhaps it already has."

CHAPTER 30

The night was long and arduous and the following day just as busy. With a massive clean-up required to repair the small town from the damage caused by the flash flood, the townsfolk pitched in and worked hard.

Gillies Bridge, the route out of town on Mount Ingalls Road going towards Corella and Boggabri, would take weeks to restore to working order. Two wooden piers had been structurally damaged by an unmanned tractor swept along in the violent flow and several metres of the timber deck had collapsed into the river below.

During what had remained of the night, Abby had assisted in moving the tourists and those living in the caravan park over to the show-ground. The townsfolk who weren't out helping with the SES were only too willing to offer shelter and a dry place to sleep for the night to those in need.

By morning, the torrent had eased to a sluggish swell and the water levels had stabilised. After downing yet another mug of coffee, Abby door-knocked checking on the elderly. Next, Abby spent several fraught hours with AJ and Riley scouring both sides of the river bank, ensuring no one else had been caught up in the powerful surge of water as it had roared down from the tablelands. Together they'd pulled two dead cows and three dead sheep from the swollen river and after Riley had photographed their brands, he'd organised for Grady Flannigan to use his bull-dozer to bury the bodies in a nearby paddock.

Every hour or so, Abby checked in with Roman. His voice, even after the long night and day, sounded firm and steady. Abby was pleased to hear the boys had had some kip on the SES bunks and were pulling their weight at the station.

They were good kids. Being here in Bindarra Creek had done them the world of good. They were thriving and loving small-town life. Wrenching them back into the world of foster care would probably have devastating effects on them.

And me, she finally admitted.

Gloria's story played over and over inside Abby's head. She recalled what Elizabeth had said about not always getting what you wanted out of life. That terrifying moment when she'd realised Drew and Eddie were trapped in a sinking car was carved into her memory.

She'd almost lost them.

She'd almost lost Roman.

Could she make this work?

And if she chose this life, would Roman play a part? Or would he return to his adrenaline fuelled career? More than once, he'd indicated he would leave his job. But she couldn't forget how he'd walked out before when their life was at its lowest.

Ten minutes ago, Riley had declared there was nothing left to do that couldn't wait until morning and locked the police station. He'd remain on-call for the night, taking the paddy wagon to his house, and he insisted both AJ and Abby go home.

After saying goodbye, Abby hauled on her coat and set off for the SES station.

As she made her weary way along Church Street, she passed the cemetery on her right. Pamela Brown was there, placing flowers on two gravestones lying side by side. Next to her, stood Roy Towns. They bowed their heads for a moment before walking away, hand-in-hand.

Feeling uplifted by the sight, Abby turned into Wattle Drive and entered the SES car park.

The place had been transformed. People marched to and fro, off-loading donations from the boots of their cars or backs of their utes and stacking the piles of clothes, blankets and canned food inside the station. The scent of cooking sausages mingled with hearty pea and ham soup wafting from two tents; one manned by Tessa, Florrie and a bewildered looking Jonas Miller, and the other by Mrs Brown's sister, her Asian husband, Mrs Cornwall and Esther Ainslie. Thea and Stavros were in the process of packing up a coffee van with plastic cups and water urns.

Abby's tummy turned over, and she hastily sat down in a nearby camp chair. Fatigue crashed into her as the events of the past twenty-four hours finally took their toll. She pressed a shaky hand to her churning belly.

"Here you go, Senior Constable. Maki thinks a nice,

warm cup of camomile and peppermint tea is what you need."

Abby looked up to find Mrs Beatrix Fukuka offering her a steaming mug. "Thank you."

Mrs Fukuka returned to clearing away the trestle table.

Taking a deep sniff, Abby drew in the calming scent, then took a few mouthfuls. Absently, she reached down and rubbed her aching knee.

"I could sleep for a week," she muttered to herself. She yawned and gazed towards the shed where Roman stood with a group of men and women. As if sensing her looking at him, he turned and lifted a hand in greeting, holding up two fingers.

Two minutes, and he'd be by her side.

From around the side of the tents strolled several young teenagers.

Abby took another sip of her tea, enjoying the sight of Drew and Eddie laughing with other kids. The boys glanced over and spotted her.

"Abby!" Eddie shouted.

She tossed her cup into a bin then rose to her feet.

He pounded across the tarmac to launch himself on her. They hugged, Abby resting her chin on his tousled hair with a deep sigh.

It felt so right.

Eddie pulled away, saying, "We've been good."

His face was earnest as he added, "And we've been helping Kaylee search for missing pets. Rufus is amazing at sniffing out other dogs and cats." He pointed to where Drew stood beside a tall, young girl with long dark hair and an elderly dog wagging his tail close to her legs.

Edwina called the kids over to the tents, where she began to hand out cold drinks.

Drew grinned and waved at Abby. He made as if to rush forward but then held back. His gaze switched to his younger brother leaning against Abby's side. The lost expression spreading over his face, just about broke her heart.

"Can we go home now?" begged Eddie. "I'm tired and want to make sure Pinky is okay."

Before she could respond, Roman strode over and lifted her hand to his lips. He kissed her knuckles. "Good question, Eddie. Can we go home?" Cocking his head to the side, he smiled.

Abby could have melted on the spot. Still, what did his words mean?

Suddenly, she needed to know, now, everything, no more doubting or wondering. This had to be settled once and for all.

"You look like hell," Roman said, cheerfully.

"Likewise." She examined the bump on the side of his head, his cut forehead, and the welt along the line of his neck visible above his jacket collar. Dark shadows smudged beneath his grey eyes, accentuating their pure silver. Were the laughter lines about his mouth deeper?

"But still beautiful." His grip on her hand tightened.

She grimaced. "I doubt it."

"No, seriously Abby. You always look beautiful to me." His words rang rich with sincerity.

"And me," inserted Eddie.

Blinking against the sting in her eyes, she averted her gaze.

"There's only ever been you. I mean it, Abby. Will you

take me home? Take all of us home?" His voice reached down deep inside her and released all those memories she'd worked so hard to contain.

The good times, the bad.

The hopes and dreams.

The images of a tiny baby cradled in her arms.

They fluttered around her mind.

Then they seemed to fade into the distance while other, more recent memories took their place. All of them gathered around the breakfast table, the boys squabbling and teasing each other. Watching the boys play soccer. The laughter as they all raced kayaks down the river. The way Drew tucked his hand under his cheek as he slept and how Eddie sprawled on his back, arms and legs wide. That amazing feeling of coming home each night after work and seeing the lights shining, hearing cheerful voices filling the house … She was astonished at how many memories there were.

And there could be more.

All she had to do was let go.

She drew a shuddering breath.

Still, she tried to laugh off the serious moment, delay when the decision was made for all time. "You're the one with the car."

For a second time, he grazed his lips over her bruised knuckles. "But you're the one who has to decide. I should never have left you, I'm sorry."

"So am I," she whispered. After a quick glance at Eddie and Drew, she led Roman a few steps away from them. They stopped near the back of a large van, well out of hearing from anyone passing by.

Taking a deep breath, she admitted, "I wanted a baby

of my own so much. I couldn't have the happiness and joy, and I couldn't let go of the grief and anger. It was the only way I had of hanging onto our child even though it never existed."

"I know, honey, I know. I'm so sorry I couldn't give you a baby of our own."

She smiled sadly and touched his face. "So am I, Roman. But it wasn't just you; it was both of us."

"If I hadn't left you …"

"Hey, I understood your need to be involved in the search for those poor people. But I admit, I was bitter that your job always seemed to come first. And that you never even considered not going to Nepal. Our adoption application had just been rejected. I felt betrayed that you didn't stay."

"I couldn't face you. I felt like I'd failed you as a man and as a husband. When I'd learned we were rejected because of my connection with a criminal, well, I felt even more at fault. Took me a while to forgive myself and realise I was a fool. You're not the only one who had difficulty letting go."

"Oh, Roman. I've never doubted you as a man." She placed a tender kiss to his lips.

"But it was more than that, Abby. I wanted to escape from the pain, the depression and all that hidden resentment building between us. That message I sent saying how I was over it all, that was wrong. What I was over was the distance between us and my guilt. If only you knew how many times I was on the point of picking up the phone and asking if we could try again. Pride held me back. Pride and fear that you'd reject me because of the selfish way I'd behaved." His lips compressed. Tears glistened in his eyes.

"No, you were right, Roman. I was obsessed but couldn't see it. I think we needed some distance for a while from each other as well as what had happened in our lives."

"I won't ever leave you again, Abby. I'm here for the long haul. Even if you decide you won't give us another chance, I'm not going to be far away. You need me, and I'll be here."

Abby smiled, her gaze straying to where Drew and Eddie waited. "We both used excuses, other reasons, blamed each other for something that was never meant to be. But look where it's led us."

Roman gently nudged her face back towards him. "Where we're meant to be?" he said, hope thickening his voice.

Abby laughed through her tears and flung her hands around his neck to hug him. She stepped back, saying, "Exactly. Come on. It's time I took you home."

Looking at the two boys standing patiently, longing etched in the anxiety on their faces, she opened her arms and said, "Welcome to the family."

Whooping, Drew and Eddie raced over to be embraced by both of them.

Then Abby took them home.

EPILOGUE

"Okay, hon. It's showtime." Roman's hands slid away from her face.

"Surprise!" roared what sounded like a crowd of people.

Opening her eyes, Abby gasped as her gaze took in her friends and the multi-tiered birthday cake with pink and gold frosting. "Roman. This is wonderful. And check out that cake!"

"Have to celebrate your birthday in style, babe. Now about that cake. Wait until you taste it. Chocolate mud cake layered with vanilla sponge, and Nutella whipped cream fudge in the middle." Pride rang loud in his voice.

"I want to eat it now." Her mouth watered as she placed Pinky on the ground. The little dog immediately trotted over to Drew, who scooped her up in his arms.

"Sorry, babe. You have to wait until we light the candles." Roman spun her around to face him and nudged her chin with his knuckles. "Happy fortieth birthday, my lovely wife."

Lowering his head, he took his time giving her a kiss that both seared her soul and filled her heart with love.

A wild burst of clapping made Abby recall she was surrounded by people, people who she'd grown closer to over the past few weeks, some she'd grown to love more than she'd believed possible. She leaned back in Roman's arms and smiled. "Thank you."

"I think we should thank each other. We've learnt from our mistakes, Abby and given *'us'* another chance." His hands slid away to indicate their friends.

And their new family.

Drew and Eddie.

They were already running back to their mates, clambering around a tree-house only partially completed. Eddie climbed up the rope ladder to where Drew had reached the timber floor built over two sturdy tree branches. Drew squatted and picked up a large piece of paper to study Roman's and his designs for the tree house.

Their friends began lining up to take turns on the flying fox Roman had made. Dodge stood by, supervising and calling instructions. At the bottom of the tree, Pinky barked then raced off following Ethan as he hurtled down the flying fox.

"We'll make it this time, Roman," she vowed.

"I know we will, babe."

A brisk wind blew over the paddock, ruffling the edges of the checked tablecloth crammed with plates of delicious food and the birthday cake.

Now that the *'surprise'* aspect of the party was over, their friends drifted away to chat in groups or help themselves to lunch. Edwina Lette and her cronies were milling about near a smaller table where a hot-water urn and tea and coffee facilities had been placed. Even the reverend was here, safely ensconced in a camp chair and chatting to Natalie Wasson and Dan and Alice Molyneaux and eating a slice of Roman's roasted pumpkin and ricotta quiche. Quite a large number of SES members with their families had turned up, as well as Riley and his wife, Sam, the Sarge bouncing a baby girl on his knee, and AJ, talking to a very pregnant, young, Indian woman holding hands with a blond-haired bloke.

"That must be AJ's eldest sister, Delhi. His mother, Gloria, told me she's about to be married and expecting a child."

"Speaking of which or whom, I should say, check out the mayor." Roman's breath feathered across her cheek as he leaned close to speak.

Abby followed the direction of his pointing finger and there was Mayor Donaldson, tan Akubra planted over his thinning brown hair, gently pushing his wife, Gloria, on a tyre-swing. There was such an air of peace emanating from the older couple that tears sprang to Abby's eyes.

Roman's fingers found hers and they interlocked. "And have you heard? Pamela Brown and Roy Towns are getting married. We're invited. Hell, I think most of the town is invited."

"That has to be the best birthday present ever." She laughed and gave him another hug.

Roman hustled off to a camp chair and began rummaging in his backpack. "Let's take some photos. First, I want a group photo."

"What? Of everyone?" Abby grinned. "You are going to need one, really big wide-angle lens."

"Oh, ye of little faith." Roman chuckled a he pulled out

his camera and began to set up his tripod. Raising his voice, he called, "Photo time! Drew! Eddie! Kids, everyone gather around the cake."

It was only a matter of minutes filled with laughter and good-natured ribbing, then they were all grouped in a semi-circle around the table. Abby was front and centre, her arms around Drew and Eddie. Their arms were about her waist, holding her tight in the same way they'd captured her heart.

Roman fiddled with the settings. "Right. That's it." He raced over, picking up Pinky as he went, and slipped in beside Abby and their boys, then yelled, "Say cheese!"

"Cheese!" Everyone laughed.

Click.

"Thanks, all. You've been a great crowd." As their friends drifted off chatting, Roman placed the little dog on the ground. Pinky raced off to sniff at Dodge's dog, Rufus, who appeared to have slept through the entire event.

"I want a photo with Abby. And the cake." Eddie swiped his finger through the icing and popped the dollop into his mouth.

"Me first. I'm the oldest." Drew elbowed his brother out of the way.

"Hey? What about a photo with me?" Roman put his hands on his hips and lifted one eyebrow.

Drew pretended to think about it. "I guess one wouldn't hurt." He grinned.

Roman put Drew in a head-lock and laughing, they wrestled each other. Then Eddie jumped on Roman's back with a wild yell.

Laughing, Abby dug out her mobile and took photo after photo of her new family.

The End

Thank you so much for taking the time to read my story *Take Me Home* which is part of the multi-author group writing venture - **Bindarra Creek A Town Reborn series**.

I hope you enjoyed reading how Abby found the inspiration and courage to let go of the past and move on to a new and wonderful future with Roman and the boys.

If you enjoyed this small town romance, check out the other books written by me in this world – *Bindarra Creek Makeover*, *Love's Sweet Challenge*, *A Dangerous Secret*, *The Mistletoe Wish* and *The Glitter or The Gold* – as well as my **Edge of the Outback** romance series.

Until next time.

BINDARRA CREEK ROMANCE SERIES

Welcome to Bindarra Creek, a struggling country town where people work hard and love deeply. Set in the picturesque tablelands of New England, Australia, Bindarra Creek is a fictional, drought stricken community full of intrigue, adventure, drama and romance.
Life and love in a small country town has never been more challenging.

Bindarra Creek A Town Reborn series consists of eight romances written by eight Australian authors and published individually (beginning in July 2019).
In order of release:
Take Me Home – Suzanne Gilchrist (aka S E Gilchrist)
In the Heat of the Night – Susanne Bellamy
No Looking Back - Linda Charles
Worth the Wait – Annie Seaton
With Every Breath – Lauren K. McKellar

BINDARRA CREEK ROMANCE SERIES

Stealing Her Heart – Simone Angela
A Twist of Fate – Erin Moira O'Hara
Promise Me Forever – Juanita Kees

৯

There are several multi-author 'series' set in our fictional small town of Bindarra Creek all written by best-selling Australian romance authors. This book is part of the A **Town Reborn** series.

Our first series, **A Bindarra Creek Romance,** was released during 2015/2016.
A collection of short romances, **Bindarra Creek Short & Sweet,** were released in January 2019.
A Town Reborn series was released during 2019/2020.
Bindarra Creek Mystery Romances were released during 2022/2023.
Bindarra Creek Christmas Romances came out in December 2022.
Bindarra Creek Small Town Christmas romances are due for release December 2023.

All books are available as ebooks, some are available also as paperbacks.

Every book can be read as a stand alone, however reading the series as a whole will give you more insight into our fictional community as the town continues to grow and change. There is drama, suspense, mystery and just simply feel-good clean and wholesome romance.

BINDARRA CREEK ROMANCE SERIES

For more info on Bindarra Creek Romances, visit www.bindarracreekromance.com

ACKNOWLEDGMENTS

Thank you to Lauren of Creating Ink for her wonderful editing services. Thank you to Patti of Paradox Book Designs for my lovely cover and for 'branding' this series.

And a special thankyou to my fellow members of this third round of Bindarra Creek Romance series – it's been an absolute pleasure to share this particular journey with all of you.

www.ingramcontent.com/pod-product-compliance
Lightning Source LLC
Chambersburg PA
CBHW071903290426
44110CB00013B/1260